Word and Spirit

Word and Spirit

CALVIN'S DOCTRINE OF BIBLICAL AUTHORITY

H. Jackson Forstman

STANFORD UNIVERSITY PRESS

STANFORD, CALIFORNIA

1962

Stanford University Press
Stanford, California

Acknowledgment

For the conception and execution of this work I am particularly indebted to the wise counsel and scholarly guidance of Professor Wilhelm Pauck of the Union Theological Seminary in New York City, from whom many have learned to admire the Protestant Reformers while exercising their critical capacities to the fullest.

H. J. F.

Stanford University
June 15, 1961

Contents

PART III. Word

Word and Spirit

Introduction

Two imposing movements in theological scholarship prompted an interest in the subject of this essay. In the field of historical research there has been a renaissance of Reformation studies. Critical editions of the reformers' works have appeared. This coupled with the critical historical method of study has given the movement an unprecedented development. The predominant currents in contemporary theology have also been a contributory factor to the vigorous interest in the two main figures of the sixteenth-century Reformation. Indeed, the new appreciation for such doctrines as justification by faith, original sin, and the sovereignty of God as well as a vigorous Christocentrism and a serious study of the Bible as the word of God have done a great deal toward pointing scholars back to the period of the Reformation.

Almost without exception the theologians who have come into prominence since the First World War have made serious efforts to be biblical theologians. Once again systems of theology have begun with the doctrine of authority or of revelation. Despite the fact that the spotlights have once more focused on the Bible— perhaps because of this—the problem of authority in the Christian faith looms as the major problem of the present day. A few years ago Robert S. Bilheimer of the World Council of Churches acknowledged this fact. Speaking at a luncheon at the Union Theological Seminary in New York City he indicated that the commission on faith and order has come to realize that a thorough discussion of the question of authority stands between the World Council and any further advancement in theological conversations. For the next few years, he predicted, this question will be central in all discussions of the World Council study program.

The problem as it has taken shape is, what is the nature of the authority of the Bible? It can readily be seen how such a problem would point men back to the Reformation, for it was there that the sole authority of scripture became the battle cry, and on that the foundation was laid for the unique place given to the Bible in Protestant Christianity. One of the most fruitful methods of preparation for a full comprehension of the many dimensions of the problem of the authority of scripture in the present day is to analyze in detail the work of those who have built their theological work on the premise of the full authority of scripture. Such a meticulous study of John Calvin's work should be particularly helpful. The nature of his writings makes possible a rather complete understanding of his view. He was both a systematizer and a biblical exegete. He discusses the doctrine of the authority of the Bible, and if there is any uncertainty about his meaning or if there is any question concerning the ramifications of his doctrine the point can be pursued by a close analysis of his application of the doctrine in the development of other doctrines and in his comments on biblical passages.

Calvin research has uniformly recognized the importance to Calvin of the authority of scripture. Indeed, there are few works dealing with the theology of this reformer which do not include a discussion of his understanding of the Bible. At the beginning of this century there appeared a monograph dealing exclusively with Calvin's view of the scriptures (Gauteron, *L'Autorité de la Bible d'après Calvin*). This short work illustrates the weakness of the treatments of the problem which were to follow. It is a recapitulation of Calvin's expressed theory of the correlation of word and Spirit, but it fails to ask the more penetrating questions about what the correlation actually means, what its consequences are, and how in practice it is carried through. The author devotes the last part to a discussion of Calvin's theory of inspiration, in which he seeks to demonstrate that Calvin was not a proponent of a literal and mechanical view.

Gauteron did this thesis under the direction of Emil Doumergue, and a few years later (1910) Doumergue's fourth volume of his mammoth work, *Jean Calvin: Les hommes et les choses de son temps*, appeared. This volume deals with the theology of the reformer and includes a chapter on the Bible consisting of two parts: The Testimony of the Holy Spirit and The Holy Scripture. Again, the brevity of the chapter precludes the discussion of a number of important issues, but it is here that Doumergue argues rather convincingly that Calvin had no theory of verbal inspiration.

The question of Calvin's view of inspiration has become the focal point of debate in the various discussions of Calvin's view of the scriptures. Reinhold Seeberg (*Lehrbuch der Dogmengeschichte*) and Otto Ritschl (*Dogmengeschichte des Protestantismus*) strongly supported a dictation theory while holding that Calvin's view of God is the key to his whole system.

In the United States Benjamin B. Warfield published between 1908 and 1915 some important essays on Calvin's theology (see the collection entitled *Calvin and Calvinism*). The essay on "The Doctrine of the Knowledge of God" deals with Calvin's view of the scripture. Warfield acknowledges the work of Doumergue, but he also sees some of the evidence to which Doumergue closed his eyes. As a result, Warfield's interpretation of Calvin is well balanced, with one exception: He is inclined to make too much of the place of reason in Calvin's theology. Even on this point, however, Warfield's interpretation is a leveling influence since most Calvin scholars minimize the role of reason in Calvin's work. Warfield's work set the pattern for the more conservative wing of the reformed tradition in America. His interpretation of Calvin has recently been echoed by Kenneth S. Kantzer in an essay entitled "Calvin and the Holy Scriptures" (*Inspiration and Interpretation*, edited by John F. Walvoord).

In 1922 a little book by Hermann Bauke appeared, *Die Probleme der Theologie Calvins*. Bauke sought to solve the enigma of Calvin's theology by claiming that it is not to be understood in terms of one central doctrine to which all others are related and from which they are derived. Rather the key is to be found in the formal structure which Bauke describes in terms of Calvin's rationalism, his use of the *complexio oppositorum* and his biblicism (formal more than material). Bauke's description of the biblical principle in Calvin's work is particularly penetrating. Unfortunately his work is more a discussion of the Calvin research than of the primary source material.

At any rate Bauke's suggestions did not take hold. Scholars

have continued the search for the unifying principle in Calvin's theology. Such an attempt was that of Wilhelm Niesel in *Die Theologie Calvins* (Munich: Chr. Kaiser Verlag, 1938, translated under the title *The Theology of Calvin*). Niesel thought he found the key to Calvin's theology in his Christocentrism. A formidable case can, of course, be summoned for this view. The question is whether it can cover the many facets of Calvin's teaching. Nonetheless, the work does serve to focus attention on the important place in Calvin's theology given to redemption, mercy, and the gracious goodness of God.

This fact, however, was made clear more than a decade before Niesel's work in the excellent study by Peter Brunner, *Vom Glauben bei Calvin*. Brunner carefully elucidates Calvin's teaching on faith, setting it in the context of the whole of the theology, thereby making clear the crucial importance of the doctrine for the full sweep of Calvin's theology. A similar task was accomplished by Edward A. Dowey, Jr., in his book, *The Knowledge of God in Calvin's Theology*. Dowey treats the *Institutes of the Christian Religion* in terms of the twofold knowledge of God (Creator and Redeemer), asserting that the organization of the work into four books is somewhat misleading. His discussion of the knowledge of God the Redeemer is exceptionally good, involving a detailed analysis of Calvin's definition of faith and issuing in the summation of our knowledge of God the Redeemer as gratuitous goodness.

In these rather representative pieces a new trend in Calvin research is noticeable. There is a new appreciation for Calvin's understanding of the love and goodness of God, and along with that for the dynamic element in Calvin's theology as a whole. Such works as those by T. F. Torrance (*Calvin's Doctrine of Man*), T. H. L. Parker (*The Doctrine of the Knowledge of God*), and Ronald S. Wallace (*Calvin's Doctrine of Word and Sacrament*) are representative of this general trend.

In most of these studies there is some discussion of Calvin's understanding of the authority of the Bible. The positions taken fall more or less into three categories. The key to the categorization is the exposition of Calvin's view of inspiration. As far as

Calvin's theory is concerned, this point demands more assumptions from the scholar than almost any other. Calvin did not develop in any one place a thorough discussion of inspiration. (See Chapter IV.) Some scholars are the children of Doumergue. That is, they minimize the evidence for a mechanical dictation theory of inspiration and concentrate on the contrary evidence. These men also tend to make much over the dynamic work of the Holy Spirit in Calvin's correlation of word and Spirit. There are variations of emphasis, to be sure, but for the most part the discussions by Parker, Niesel, and Wallace show affinities in this respect. The works of J. K. S. Reid (*The Authority of Scripture: A Study of the Reformation and Post-Reformation Understanding of the Bible*), Henri Clavier (*Études sur le Calvinisme*), and Hermann Noltensmeier (*Reformatorische Einheit: Das Schriftverständnis bei Luther und Calvin*) also may be classed here. Clavier is closest to Doumergue; Reid uses the Barthian notion of the Bible as witness to the revelation in contradistinction to being the revelation itself; and Noltensmeier points out the similarities between the two reformers on the doctrine of the scriptures.

Seeberg and Ritschl, it has been pointed out, understood Calvin to believe in verbal inspiration. More in line with these two than with any others is Rupert E. Davies in his essay *The Problem of Authority in the Continental Reformers*. It is characteristic of this position that Davies makes little out of Calvin's statements on the work of the Holy Spirit.

A third position shows some affinities with the interpretation of Warfield, who, although he acknowledged Doumergue's arguments, insisted that Calvin was a biblicist and took the entire Bible as the word of God. Both E. A. Dowey, Jr., and Brian A. Gerrish ("Biblical Authority and the Continental Reformation") reflect a certain duality in Calvin's thought on the problem. It is interesting that both men quote Warfield favorably.

In all of these works the discussion of Calvin's conception of authority is only incidental to the study as a whole or, as in the case of Davies and Reid, only a part of a more comprehensive study. Consequently, they must inevitably be cursory and, insofar as the problem of authority is concerned, neglect some penetrating questions. There is always the possibility of missing the full meaning of Calvin's view when it is not pursued to the extent of its actual application.

This is often the weakness of present-day discussions of the problem of authority. For example, a rather satisfying position can be built around the claim that the Bible is witness to the revelation while it is not the revelation itself. Ostensibly, this relieves one of the intolerable charge, "Paper Pope," while it maintains the security of the authority of the Bible. But the most pressing question is, What precisely does this mean, and how does it work out in relation to specific passages of scripture? This was one of the issues raised by Reinhold Niebuhr in his exchange with Karl Barth in *The Christian Century* (1948–49; see Bibliography). In those articles Barth's answers were not entirely clear and satisfactory.

The purpose of this essay is not only to describe Calvin's conception of the authority of the Bible, but also to ask the question, What does it mean? and to evaluate how the conception actually works out. Consequently, Part I deals with the theory as a whole, its theological foundations and dominating prominence in the entire work of the Genevan Reformer. In Part II the one side of the correlation is investigated. The precise nature of the work of the Holy Spirit in the writers of the Bible and in believers is sought after. Part III deals with the word, the other side of the correlation of authority. This involves a more detailed analysis of the content and character of knowledge, of Calvin's exegesis and of the nature of certainty which pervades Calvin's thought and life. The conclusion will discuss some of the strands of Calvin's thought picked up in later Calvinism and something of the relevance of Calvin's thought to contemporary discussion of the problem of authority.

PART I

Calvin's Doctrine
of Authority

Theological Foundations
for Calvin's Understanding
of Authority

John Calvin was a man obsessed with a desire to know, "tormented by an incomparable need for certitude," as Emil Doumergue has put it.[1] This need was satisfied only when he found what he considered to be the authoritative source of knowledge. It will be the task of this essay to expound Calvin's understanding of the authoritative source of knowledge and to show in what ways and to what purposes he put it to use in his systematic and exegetical work.

That it is knowledge in which Calvin is primarily interested is clear from the beginning of his most famous work, *Institutes of the Christian Religion,** where he writes, "True and substantial wisdom principally consists of two parts, the knowledge of God, and the knowledge of ourselves (*Dei cognitione et nostri*)."[2] The exposition of the knowledge of God and self is, in the most general view, Calvin's theological work. Most certainly this double knowledge, as Calvin understands it, both poses the problem and sets the boundaries for his conception of authority. His view of God is so high and his view of man so low that the problem of the communication of knowledge is severe. On the other hand, because of this the solution of the problem must be in radical terms of the self-communication of God to man, else it will not be authoritative.

---

[1] Numbered notes (primarily source citations) will be found at the back of the book, on pages 157–66.

* It is, indeed, evident in the title itself. *Institutio* means instruction. It also means arrangement. Calvin intended the *Institutes* to be an orderly arrangement of the available and important knowledge of the Christian faith. See Author's Preface to the 1559 edition of the *Institutes.* Allen, pp. 18–19; O.S. III. 6.18–7.1.

When Calvin speaks of God it is in terms of the divine majesty. This majesty is beyond our highest conceptions. We can only speak of the "infinite fulness of God,"[3] and "acknowledge that in the Lord alone are to be found true wisdom, solid strength, perfect goodness, and unspotted righteousness."[4] A number of Calvin interpreters have argued that the key to his theology is to be found in the overarching sovereignty of God. They are right in the sense that the tone of the active divine majesty sounded so firmly by Calvin at the beginning of the *Institutes* is maintained with an overwhelming consistency throughout the whole of his work.

In fact, as it turns out, this understanding of God is the necessary prerequisite for that other branch of "true and substantial wisdom," the knowledge of ourselves. At first Calvin indicates that a work such as the *Institutes* could begin with an exposition of either the knowledge of self or the knowledge of God. Every man should be able to recognize his own poverty and to derive from that a conception of the perfections of God.[5] "The knowledge of ourselves, therefore, is not only an incitement to seek after God, but likewise a considerable assistance towards finding him."[6] This imperfection, however, which any man should be able to recognize, is so thoroughgoing that it obscures man to himself. The only reliable way to come to a knowledge of oneself is thus to consider the majesty of God.

> It is plain that no man can arrive at the true knowledge of himself, without having first contemplated the divine character, and then descended to the consideration of his own. For, such is the native pride (*superbia*) of us all, we invariably esteem ourselves righteous, innocent, wise, and holy, till we are convinced by clear proofs, of our unrighteousness, turpitude, folly, and impurity. But we are never thus convinced, while we confine our attention to ourselves, and regard not the Lord, who is the only standard by which this judgment ought to be formed.[7]

The knowledge of God and the knowledge of self are clearly correlates to Calvin: the one implies the other, and vice versa. Just as the fullness of God is beyond human comprehension, so Calvin finds it somewhat difficult to locate the words to describe fully the meanness of men. He speaks of our "miserable condition" which ought "to overwhelm us with shame," particularly when it is compared with the excellency of our nature as it was first created by God and the divine goodness even after our rebellion.[8] Original sin is defined by Calvin as "an hereditary pravity and corruption of our nature, diffused through all the parts of the soul, rendering us obnoxious to the Divine wrath, and producing in us those works which the Scripture calls 'works of the flesh' (Gal. 5:19)."[9]

Calvin can speak of the present condition of men as the absolute triumph of concupiscence, and it must be noted that he understands concupiscence in the wider meaning of the term. "Everything in man, the understanding and will, the soul and body is polluted and engrossed by this concupiscence; or, to express it more briefly, that man is of himself nothing else but concupiscence."[10] This, then, is the knowledge of oneself: a consciousness of one's own "calamity, poverty, nakedness, and ignominy."[11]

The Boundaries of the Doctrine of Authority

As was indicated above, this knowledge of God and of oneself has determinative implications for the understanding of authority. Calvin himself expresses the relevance of the double knowledge to the necessity of authority. "For, till men are sensible that they owe every thing to God (an awareness dependent on both the knowledge of self and of God), that they are supported by his paternal care, that he is the Author of all the blessings they enjoy, and that nothing should be sought independently of him, they will never voluntarily submit to his authority."[12] The knowledge of God and self inevitably leads one to submit to God's authority.* "For how can you entertain a thought of God without immediately reflecting that, being a creature of his formation, you must, by right of creation, be subject to his authority."[13]

What then are the implications of this double knowledge for

---

* It ought to be observed that Calvin thought the Bible was the only final authoritative source for a knowledge of God and self. The knowledge and the authority, then, are inseparably bound together so that it is difficult to say which comes first. However, this does not deter him from separating them on occasion as he does here.

the conception of authority? In the first place, if there is to be any authoritative and sufficient knowledge, it will have to come at the divine initiative. To be sure, Calvin discusses the possibility of a natural knowledge of God and self in the first few chapters of Book I in the *Institutes*. Abstractly considered, the breadth of the knowledge of God the Creator available to one who reflects on the nature of man and the world is striking.[14] In reality, however, man is now incapable of reading this revelation of God in the creation. He is too stupid to derive any benefit from such "obvious testimonies."[15] Xenophon related Socrates' praise of Apollo because he taught that men should worship the gods according to the ways prescribed by their own country or city. Calvin comments, "Who could so acquiesce in the decrees of the rulers or the ordinances of the people, as without hesitation to receive a god delivered to him by the authority of man?" He concludes, "It remains for God himself to give a revelation concerning himself from heaven."[16] If left to themselves, men are utterly lost because the knowledge of God is far beyond their reach. "And certainly the knowledge of God (*cognitio Dei*) is a wisdom that is too high for our attaining it by our own acuteness, and our weakness shews itself in daily instances in our own experience, when God withdraws his hand for a little while."[17] The authoritative knowledge of God must come through the self-communication of God himself.

In the second place, because God is, in the strict sense, incomprehensible, no authority will be able to communicate fully all the mysteries of God. There will be a good deal that must remain unknown to mortal men. In his discussion of faith in the *Institutes* Calvin is militantly polemical against the Roman Catholic conception of implicit faith, but after making it clear that faith implies knowledge* he goes on to admit that in one sense faith is implicit. This implicit element has to do with the essence and the mysteries of God which no man could possibly understand because of his ignorance as well as the fact that he is bounded by the flesh. "I do not deny (such is the ignorance with which we are enveloped) that many things are very obscure to us at present, and will continue

---

* III. ii. 2 (O.S. IV. 10.11–12). "Faith consists not in ignorance, but in knowledge."

to be so, till we shall have cast off the burden of the flesh, and arrived nearer to the presence of God. On such subjects, nothing would be more proper than a suspension of judgment, and a firm resolution to maintain unity with the Church."[18]

Calvin wants all men to see the sufficiency of what God has communicated to us. No man should try to go beyond that. The doctrine of creation, for example, shows what happens when men give vent to speculation. There are all sorts of monstrous fables which try to explain the creation, the best of which is "utterly vain and worthless."[19] In order to lift man from this morass of error God communicated to him a history of the creation. This history serves both to dispel false notions about the creation and to set bounds to the questions one can legitimately ask concerning the creation. "Great shrewdness was discovered by a certain pious old man, who, when some scoffer ludicrously inquired what God had been doing before the creation of the world, replied that he had been making hell for over curious men."[20]

The case is clear: Because man is what he is and because God is what he is, even a reliable authority will not be able to comprehend God in his essence. A man should simply recognize this and accept his limitations. As Calvin put it, "Let no man hesitate to acknowledge, that he is incapable of understanding the mysteries of God, any further than he has been illuminated by Divine grace. He who attributes to himself more understanding, is so much the blinder, because he does not perceive and acknowledge his blindness."[21]

If it be true that a man can never know all about the essence of God as long as he is bounded by the ignorance and finitude of the flesh, and if we keep in mind the infinite distance between the majesty of God and the meanness of men, then we may see further that what knowledge of the infinite God is communicated to men will of necessity be tempered to the human capacity. In Calvin's theology this is the principle of accommodation. It is perhaps his most widely used exegetical tool. The *locus classicus* is a passage from the chapter on the Trinity in the *Institutes:*

> For who, even of the meanest capacity, understands not, that God lisps, as it were, with us, just as nurses are accustomed to speak to infants? Wherefore, such forms of expression

[that God has mouth, ears, eyes, hands, and feet] do not clearly explain the nature of God, but accommodate (*accommodant*) the knowledge of him (*eius notitiam*) to our narrow capacity; to accomplish which, the Scripture must necessarily descend far below the height of his majesty.[22]

The principle of accommodation means to Calvin not only that God will have to lisp, so to speak, but that his lisping must be written down in a permanent record. The uselessness of a natural theology, given man's condition of distorting ignorance, has been briefly mentioned. The revelation in creation is there, but men cannot see it for what it is. They are therefore like old men whose eyes, having grown dim with age, require the use of spectacles in order to read the pages of a book. The only way one can clearly and truly see God in the creation and draw the right conclusions about the revelation in creation is with the aid of the scriptures.[23] It is quite important that the full scope of the truth which God has communicated to men be made available to all ages. For this purpose God determined that his oracles "be committed to public records."[24]

> For, if we consider the mutability of the human mind,—how easy its lapse into forgetfulness of God; how great its propensity to errors of every kind; how violent its rage for the perpetual fabrication of new and false religions,—it will be easy to perceive the necessity of the heavenly doctrine being thus committed to writing, that it might not be lost in oblivion, or evaporate in error, or be corrupted by the presumption of men.[25]

Accommodation does not mean that the revelation in the Bible is truth mixed with foreign matter. What is in the Bible is pure. Because all men are mean, ignorant, and utterly incapable of comprehending God, not only must the true revelation come from God himself, but since it must be communicated to men through human channels (namely, a book written by human hands), the human element must be overcome. There are times when Calvin is willing to admit a human element in the scriptures (as, for example, in the exegesis of Jeremiah 15:18), but he will insist that it has nothing at all to do with the doctrine.[26]

For though the prophet announced nothing human (*nihil humanum attulit*) when he declared the truth of God, yet he was not wholly exempt from sorrow and fear and other feelings of the flesh. For we must always distinguish, when we speak of the prophets and the apostles, between the truth (*inter ipsam doctrinam*), which was pure, free from every imperfection, and their own persons (*inter ipsorum personas*), as they commonly say, or themselves.

He goes on to say that none of the writers was so perfectly renewed that all remnants of the flesh were swept away, and in this instance Jeremiah was, as is so often the case with men, overcome with weariness and anxiety. "He was then subject to these feelings, that is, as to himself; yet his doctrine was free from every defect, for the Holy Spirit guided his mind, his thoughts, and his tongue, so that there was in it nothing human."*

Given the understanding of God and man, if we are to have a trustworthy source of knowledge it must be clear that the source is divine. "Faith can rest on no other foundation than his eternal veracity (*quam in aeterna eius veritate*)."[27] One might further say that faith is founded not only on the true God but also on the fact that the true God is truly communicated. Thus we must know that what is proposed to us in the Bible "has proceeded from his sacred mouth (*ex sacro eius ore*)."[28] Calvin considers this to be one of the principles which distinguish the Christian religion from all other religions and a point about which there can be no debate. "We know (*scimus*) that God hath spoken to us, and are fully convinced that the prophets did not speak at their own suggestion, but that, being organs of the Holy Spirit (*sed ut erant spiritus sancti organa*), they only uttered what they had been commissioned from heaven to declare."[29] The law and the prophets are, in short, "dictated by the Holy Spirit (*a spiritu sancto dictatam*)."[30]

In sum, it can be said that the authority of the prophets and of the other writers of the Bible, and therefore the authority of the Bible itself, depends in no way upon the men but rather depends

* Com. Jer. 15:18 (C.O. 38.231). *Interea doctrina carruit omni naevo: quia spiritus sanctus eo mentem eius et sensus omnes, et linguam sic direxit ut nihil esset illic humanum.*

entirely upon the fact that they delivered faithfully as if it were "from hand to hand, what the Lord . . . commanded them, without adding any thing whatever of their own (*et nihil prorsus addunt de suo*)."[31] The result is the certainty that the gospel is true because it has come from God rather than men.[32]

The Problem of the Doctrine of Authority

We have now seen how Calvin's understanding of God and man determines certain conditions and boundaries for the conception of authority. It means that knowledge must come at the divine initiative and that no authority can comprehend God in his essence. What knowledge is possible must be tempered to the human capacity (accommodation), and accommodation, in this instance, means a written book. That understanding also poses the problem. As for the question about how the knowledge can be communicated to special men who then can transcribe it reliably to the written page, we have just noted that Calvin introduces the agency of the Holy Spirit. There remains another facet of the same problem. Granted that the true knowledge of God and his will can be committed to writing and yet remembering Calvin's radical understanding of original sin, how can a man receive the revelation, perfect though it may be?

Calvin does not by-pass this problem. Nor does he simplify it by altering his view of man. He might have done the latter. After all, any man can read or hear the word and then decide for or against it as the word of God. Calvin's radical understanding of human impotence is consistent at this point. "Men are not capable of believing,"[33] he writes. "No man can come to faith by his own sagacity."[34] He solves the problem of the reception of the revelation in the same way in which he solved the problem of the recording of the revelation, by introducing the agency of the Holy Spirit. "The Word of God is like the sun shining on all to whom it is preached; but without any benefit to the blind. But in this respect we are all blind by nature; therefore it cannot penetrate into our minds unless the internal teacher, the Spirit, make way for it by his illumination (*interiore illo magistro Spiritu per suam illuminationem aditum faciente*)."[35]

It is possible, Calvin thinks, to derive what should be conclusive rational proofs of the divinity of scripture, thus ostensibly establishing belief. He does this in the eighth chapter of the first book in the *Institutes*. But it is important to note that this discussion comes after a chapter on the necessity of scripture to a knowledge of God the creator and another chapter on the necessity of the testimony of the Spirit for the establishment of the authority of scripture. Before the discussion on the rational proofs (the *indicia*) Calvin writes, "Now, if we wish to consult the true interest of our consciences that they may not hesitate at the smallest scruples,—this persuasion must be sought from a higher source than human reasons, or judgments, or conjectures—even from the secret testimony of the Spirit."[36] At the beginning of the discussion he makes it clear that these proofs are only of assistance when one is already certainly persuaded of the authority of scripture. He concludes his exposition of the *indicia* by asserting, "The Scripture will then only be effectual to produce the saving knowledge of God, when the certainty of it shall be founded on the internal persuasion of the Holy Spirit."[37]

In his discussion of faith in Book III the same emphasis is made, and again it is connected with his understanding of man. One ought to be able to come to faith on the basis of a simple demonstration of the word, but one's blindness and perverseness obstruct it. Man is too much given to error; he is so dull that he could never see it by himself. "Therefore nothing is effected by the word, without the illumination of the Holy Spirit."[38]

Let it be considered, then, as an undeniable truth, that they who have been inwardly taught by the Spirit (*quos Spiritus sanctus intus docuit*), feel an entire acquiescence in the Scripture (*solide acquiescere in Scriptura*), and that it is self-authenticated (*autopiston*), carrying with it its own evidence, and ought not to be made the subject of demonstration and arguments from reason; but it obtains the credit which it deserves with us by the testimony of the Spirit (*Spiritus testimonio consequi*). For though it conciliate our reverence by its internal majesty, it never seriously affects us till it is confirmed by the Spirit in our hearts (*per Spiritum obsignata est cordibus nostris*). Therefore, being illuminated by him (*Illius ergo virtute illuminati*), we now believe the divine original of the

Scripture (*a Deo esse Scripturam*), not from our own judgment or that of others, but we esteem the certainty, that we have received it from God's own mouth (*ab ipsissimo Dei ore*) by the ministry of men, to be superior to that of any human judgment, and equal to that of an intuitive perception of God himself in it. We seek not arguments or probabilities to support our judgment, but submit our judgments and understandings as to a thing concerning which it is impossible for us to judge.[39]

Although the problem of how God can communicate knowledge to man has two facets—how the revelation is recorded and how it is received by the one who reads or hears the record— it is conceived by Calvin as a single problem and is given a single solution: the agency of the Holy Spirit. "The same Spirit, therefore, who made Moses and the prophets certain of their calling, now also testifies to our hearts (*testatur cordibus nostris*) that he has employed them as his servants to instruct us (*esse ad nos docendos*)."[40]

The basic statement of Calvin's conception of authority can now be understood. Authority for the Christian faith, for the reliable knowledge of God and man, is to be found in a reciprocal relation of word and Spirit.

For the Lord hath established a kind of mutual connection between the certainty of his word and of his Spirit (*Mutuo enim quodam nexu Dominus verbi Spiritus qui sui certitudinem inter se copulari*); so that our minds are filled with a solid reverence for the word, when by the light of the Spirit we are enabled therein to behold the Divine countenance; and, on the other hand, without the least fear of mistake, we gladly receive the Spirit, when we recognize him in his image, that is, in the word.*

As we have seen that the word cannot be separated from the Spirit because man in himself is incapable of recognizing it for what it is, so also the Spirit cannot be conceived as separate from the word. This would lead to all sorts of vain imaginings of the sort Calvin knew only too well in his own day. "There are many fanatics," he writes,

* I. ix. 3 (O.S. III. 84.14–20). Cf. Com. Isa. 59:21 (C.O. 37.352): *Spiritus coniungitur verbo, quoniam sine efficacia spiritus nihil efficeret praedicatio verbi, sed maneret infructuoso*; Com. Ezek. 2:1, 2 (C.O. 40. 61, 62); II. v. 5 (O.S. III. 302–3).

who disdain the outward preaching, and talk in lofty terms about secret revelations and inspirations, (*enthousiasmous*). But we see how Christ joins these two things together; and, therefore, though there is no faith till the Spirit of God seal our minds and hearts (*nulla est fides, donec mentes nostras illustret Dei spiritus et corda obsignet*), still we must not go to seek visions or oracles in the clouds; but the word (*verbum*), which is near us, in our mouth and heart, (Rom. 10:8) must keep all our senses bound and fixed on itself.[41]

The two elements, then, are necessary to one another. The word presents us with the content of faith and knowledge. The Spirit is the internal agent by which we are enabled to believe the word. The children of God "are sensible that, exclusively of the Spirit of God, they are utterly destitute of the light of truth, yet [they] are not ignorant that the word is the instrument, by which the Lord dispenses to believers the illumination of his Spirit (*verbum esse organum quo illuminationem fidelibus Dominus dispensat*)."[42]

The full impact of such a conception of authority is an absolute certainty which towers over the vicissitudes of history and trembles not in the least at the most overwhelming human weaknesses. An authority is expounded which is dependent in no determinative way upon human beings. The authority is God. He communicates himself to prophets and apostles through the Holy Spirit, and under the overpowering influence of this Spirit these men are led to write. The collection of these writings is then recognized by men as the true knowledge of God through the internal agency of the same Holy Spirit. The writers have not ceased to be human beings, nor have those who accept their writings and believe them ceased to be men, but the human element in each instance has been so circumscribed that it is no longer a real peril to the authority.

If one can go this far with Calvin, doubt has been conquered. And Calvin himself rests fully assured in this understanding precisely because he himself as a frail human being is removed from it without being removed. He benefits from it, and finds his place within the scheme, but the scheme is in no way dependent on John Calvin. "Our doctrine," he writes, "must stand, exalted above all the glory, and invincible by all the power of the world; because

it is not ours, but the doctrine of the living God, and of his Christ."[43]
It is in this vein that, in his Open Letter to Francis I with which he
prefaced the first edition and each succeeding edition of the *Institutes*, he alluded to Paul's instruction that "every prophecy should
be framed 'according to the analogy of faith' (Rom. 12:6). Calvin was willing to rest his case on this rock.

> For what is more consistent with faith than to acknowledge
> ourselves naked of all virtue, that we may be clothed by God;
> empty of all good, that we may be filled by him; slaves to sin,
> that we may be liberated by him; blind, that we may be enlightened by him; lame, that we may be guided; weak, that we
> may be supported by him; to divest ourselves of all ground of
> glorying, that he alone may be eminently glorious, and that we
> may glory in him.[44]

This man, beginning with an understanding of God and man cast
in the most radical language and "tormented by an incomparable
need of certainty," fulfilled his quest. It issued in an understanding of authority, conceived as the interrelation of the word of
God and the Holy Spirit in which he was lifted above himself and
brought face to face with the living God.

Calvin as a Biblical Theologian

We forget to speak well when we cease to speak with God.
III. xxiii. 5 (O.S. IV. 399.27–28)

Let us, I say, permit the Christian man to open his heart
and his ears to all the discourses addressed to him by God,
only with this moderation, that as soon as the Lord closes
his sacred mouth, he shall also desist from further inquiry.
III. xxi. 3 (O.S. IV. 372.7–11)

"Man of the Book" is a cliché well nigh worn out from use by
funeral orators and overly pious and sympathetic biographers of
clergymen. It can, perhaps, be applied literally as much to Calvin
as to any other historical figure. We have seen how Calvin's fundamental theological tenets issued in a conception of authority
centering in the Bible and thoroughly alleviating, because of its
peculiar qualities, that need for certainty by which Calvin was
"tormented." We may now observe Calvin's almost inhuman consistency in carrying out this principle of authority in his life and
work.

The foundation was laid. He had dug and dug deep until he
had found the rock. The structure which he intended to raise
would not be one built upon sand, to crumble with the onslaught
of wind, rain, and flood. It would stand because it was resting in
its center and on all its corners on the almighty God himself. This
structure was to be a biblical theology full blown. One may picture it as a massive, thick-walled cathedral with two imposing
towers. The one tower represents his expositional and exegetical
work. From Calvin's lecture hall, pulpit, and study came massive

volumes of commentaries and sermons on a phenomenally large portion of the Bible. The other tower is the *Institutes,* a work which, according to Calvin's intention, should be considered as nothing other than an introduction to the study of the Bible and an orderly arrangement of the knowledge available from its pages.

> Now, my design in this work has been to prepare and qualify students of theology for the reading of the divine word, that they may have an easy introduction to it, and be enabled to proceed in it without any obstruction. For I think I have given such a comprehensive summary, and orderly arrangement of all the branches of religion, that, with proper attention, no person will find any difficulty in determining what ought to be the principal objects of his research in the Scripture, and to what end he ought to refer any thing it contains.[1]

In short, the scriptures were considered by Calvin to be sufficient, complete, and necessary. Should anyone think otherwise, not only would he be guilty of accusing the apostles of dishonesty, since Calvin understood such a passage as "He [the Holy Spirit] will lead you into all truth" (Jn. 16:13) and other passages of a similar nature as claims by the apostles to deliver the full truth of God, but he would also be subject to the charge of blasphemy because the Spirit prompted the apostles to make such claims in the first place.[2]

It is true that there are many things that are simply beyond the province of the human mind to know. In the face of these secrets beyond human comprehension one must only recognize the fact and rest assured in it "that all those who endeavour to serve him with an upright desire will be brought, by the teaching of the Holy Spirit (*Spiritus ductu*), to the knowledge of that heavenly wisdom which is appointed for their salvation."[3] Although one can never know everything, all that one needs to know can most certainly be found in that source of all Christian knowledge, the Bible. This same claim is made for Christ, but it must be understood that when Calvin limits the human scope to what Christ said, he is in effect limiting it to the Bible, inasmuch as he considered the Bible to say in an authoritative way no more than what Christ said. "It is rather necessary," he writes, "that the mouths of all men should be be shut, since he has spoken, . . . that is, has spoken in such a manner as to leave nothing to be said by others after him."[4]

Actually there are two kinds of men: those who "are actuated by an inordinate desire of knowing more than is right,"[5] and those who claim too much ignorance. Calvin considers both types in one of his discussions of election. Of the first variety he comments that when one goes beyond the boundary of the word the result will inevitably be "errors, slips, and falls." He then exhorts the reader to be content with the knowledge of predestination which is provided in the Bible and not to be ashamed of ignorance on matters "relative to a subject in which there is a kind of learned ignorance (*docta ignorantia*)."[6] To the other type he addresses a warning no less stringent. "To observe, therefore, the legitimate boundary on this side also, we must recur to the word of the Lord, which affords a certain rule for the understanding. For the Scripture is the school of the Holy Spirit, in which as nothing necessary and useful to be known is omitted, so nothing is taught which it is not beneficial to know."[7] It follows from this that the word is indispensable, and this is precisely what Calvin intends to say. "We must not seek anywhere else the wisdom which is sufficient for salvation."[8]

The Theory of the Biblical Theologian

Calvin follows his maxim on the sufficiency and necessity of the Bible both in theory and in practice. The theory he expresses by carefully considering every other claim to authority and bringing each of them to the bar of judgment by the word of God. This careful consideration should be noted. The Genevan Reformer did not simply dismiss every claim other than the Bible nor did he set those claims in opposition to the word. He could not do this because he realized that the word demanded interpretation, the work he himself set out to do. Therefore such claims to authority as the Church Fathers, the councils, pastors and teachers, the Church itself, and human reason could not be dismissed summarily. They might well be valid interpretations of the Bible.

Because of this, Calvin's remarks on claims to authority other than the Bible are occasionally surprising. At times he makes apparently sweeping statements about the authority of Augustine, or the Apostles' Creed, or the Church and its pastors. But in each instance he somewhere explicitly states, thus keeping pace with his maxim, that any of these is authoritative only because and insofar as it reflects what is stated in the word of God. This is necessary because all of these other possible authorities differ in one crucially important respect from the Bible: with them the human element is active and will surely at one point or another be determinative and productive of error.

Such a view is explicitly stated in Calvin's discussions of the authority of the Fathers. Calvin would not think of dismissing the Church Fathers *in toto*. On the contrary, he is willing, in his contest with the Roman Church, to suspend temporarily the most conclusive evidence for the dispute and argue only on the basis of the Fathers. "The victory in most parts of the controversy— to speak in the most modest terms—would be on our side."[9] But this could only be a temporary arrangement—a game of chess with the rules altered for this one occasion—for a reason above all others in John Calvin's mind: "Yet in some respects they have suffered the common fate of mankind."[10] It must be understood that it is only to Christ that the Christian owes absolute obedience,[11] and we may add that Christ can be found with certainty on all occasions only in the word.

With the Fathers, as also with the Councils, Calvin has a sense of an inequality of authority depending on age. The early Fathers and the first four ecumenical councils are to be taken more seriously than those which are not so ancient. Calvin demonstrated at this point his affinity with the humanists in their battle cry, Back to the sources! It is also an indication that Calvin participated in the budding historical consciousness of his day. Ideas and ways of understanding do change from one age to the next. The only sure way to get at the original idea or understanding is to go directly to the original source, and among secondary sources the most valuable will be those which stand nearest the original in time.

But of course, this is never, with Calvin, a guiding principle by itself. He applies it only as subsidiary to the main guide—that is, whether or not the writings of a Father or the decrees of a council agree with the word of God. In his discussion of the Trinity Calvin follows Augustine quite closely and calls attention to the fact, but he does this because, first of all, he thinks Augustine is true to the scriptures and, second, because he believes Augustine will be a useful aid for preventing the student from wandering "through a multitude of vain speculations."[12] Calvin not only is willing to accept, but also thinks all Christians should accept the decrees of the first four general councils, not because there is anything inherently sacred about those councils but rather because they "contain nothing but the pure and natural interpretation of the Scripture (*puram et naturam Scripturae interpretationem*)."[13] Earlier in the same discussion Calvin stated in characteristically strong language that councils are authoritative only when they are governed by the word and the Spirit so that their decrees differ at no point from Holy Scripture,[14] and subsequently he makes clear how one may distinguish between councils whose decrees are at variance with one another: "The only way I know, is to ascertain from the Scriptures that its [the one council's] decrees are not orthodox; for there is no other certain rule of decision."[15]

Calvin did consider the Fathers and councils authoritative to a degree. The alternative to such a position would have been to consider authoritative only one who does nothing but quote verses of scripture. This could hardly be construed as communication, but the gospel must be proclaimed and an understanding of it must be conveyed. So he upholds the attempt to understand scripture in nonscriptural terms. It is unreasonable to be regulated by the adverse principle inasmuch as it condemns all interpretation and apparently approves only the connection of detached texts.[16] One can use nonbiblical language to make clear the content of the Bible. The Apostles' Creed does this:

> But what we ought principally to regard, is beyond all controversy—that it comprehends a complete account of our faith in a concise and distinct order, and that everything it contains is confirmed by decisive testimonies of Scripture. This being

ascertained, it is of no use anxiously to inquire, or to contend with any one, respecting its author, unless it be not sufficient for any one to have the unerring truth of the Holy Spirit without knowing either by whose mouth it was uttered, or by whose hand it was written.[17]

This conviction is behind his explanation to Cardinal Sadolet of the authority he is willing to grant to Fathers and councils. "For, although we hold that the Word of God alone lies beyond the sphere of our judgment, and that Fathers and Councils are of authority only insofar as they agree with the rule of the Word, we still give to Councils and Fathers such rank and honor as it is proper for them under Christ to hold."[18] But the reservation in all instances must be kept carefully in mind.

Reason is another authority which Calvin both uses and discusses. Of course, he criticizes the human reason for seeking to know more than is in its province to penetrate. The secrets of God must remain secrets until one is divested of the flesh. This, however, should not be taken as an outright rebuff of human reason. On the contrary, Calvin makes rather astounding claims for the coherence of his theology, and only on rare occasions—and then never in an outright way—does he admit the irrationality of a position he is defending. In some of his most difficult passages, such as the discussions of the divine responsibility for human good and the human responsibility for evil, he does not make such an admission. Quite the contrary, he thinks the explanations make good sense.

The reader begins to suspect that coherent rationality carries a good deal of weight with Calvin when at the beginning of his appeal to Francis I he pleads for a reasonable hearing, asking that Francis try to understand his position.[19] Calvin mentions that his adversaries claim his pleading the word is a vain pretension. On this he comments that Francis in his wisdom will be able to judge for himself upon reading the confession (the *Institutes*).[20] In such a statement as this it would seem that Calvin sees the truth as something objective that can be judged by objective norms.

This may certainly be taken as a plea for clear and honest thinking, but it cannot be construed as a defense of reason as an

independent authority. The "reason" which Calvin claims to have
on his side against the Roman Catholics is not by any means a
reason free from presuppositions. Rather it is a plea for the use
of good reason as a tool in handling the content of our faith which
is to be found in the word of God.

Even this use of reason is limited, however, and the limitation
is to be found in the word itself. One finds in the Commentary on
Joshua one of the few places where Calvin admits that one's reason
might be offended by something in the scriptures. It is in the exegesis of one of the several passages dealing with the wholesale
slaughter of men, women, and children by the Hebrews during the
occupation of the Promised Land. Some might find it difficult to
reconcile such brutality as a command of God with the assertion
of the overarching goodness of God. If such a problem does arise,
then one must call a halt to his reasoning and acquiesce.

> If any one is disturbed and offended by the severity of the
> punishment, he must always be brought back to this point,
> that though our reason (*ratio nostra*) dissent from the judg-
> ments of God, we must check our presumption by the curb of
> a pious modesty and soberness, and not disapprove whatever
> does not please us. . . . If we consider how much more deeply
> divine knowledge penetrates than human intellect can possibly
> do (*Dei cognitio quam mentes nostrae intelligentia*), we will
> rather acquiesce in his decree, than hurry ourselves to a preci-
> pice by giving way to presumption and extravagant pride.[21]

Reason must remain subject to the word.

Having made this point, however, it would be unwise to neglect the force upon Calvin's self-consciousness wielded by his belief that reason was on his side. Given the uncompromising bias
against speculation, and acknowledging the weakness of a good
deal of what Calvin passed off as conclusive arguments, yet the
very fact that Calvin himself considered his arguments sound and
his doctrine coherent had the effect of a steel support to the walls
of his cathedral. Nor is this to deny that the walls had no need of
steel support. The word can stand alone against all onslaughts,
but when the early Fathers and the councils and, most particularly,
clear thought and rational coherency stand behind the word, the

overall effect is an incredible certainty, the total impact of which constituted the inner dynamic in Calvin's self-consciousness.

If the reader of Calvin is called upon to evaluate the Reformer's normative statements on behalf of creeds, Fathers, councils, and reason, then he must certainly take pause when he considers Calvin's statements about the Church and its pastors. "We are certain," he writes, "as long as we continue in the bosom of the Church, that we shall remain in possession of the truth."[22] The article in the Apostles' Creed which we know as "I believe in the Church," Calvin reads as "I believe the Church."[23] This is taken to refer to the authority of the Church.[24] So far as the visible Church is concerned, Calvin thinks there is no better term on which to fix the attention than the word "Mother," for there is no other entrance into life. "We must continue under her instruction and discipline to the end of our life."[25] As a matter of fact, "God has not promised to impart his mercy, except in the communion of saints."[26]

Calvin writes in this same vein about the leaders of the Church. When they declare a sentence, "God has testified that it is no other than a declaration of his sentence, and that what they do on earth shall be ratified in heaven."[27] It is asserted that Christ has appointed this particular order for his Church because he is not here to express his will.[28] This, in effect, says that the officers of the Church *do* express his will. This fact becomes quite clear when preaching is considered. For God has connected preaching with his Spirit.[29] This is almost equal to saying that when one who has been properly ordained and appointed to preach stands up to discharge his office, it is not he who speaks but the Holy Spirit who speaks through him.

But not quite, or rather, not necessarily. Even the authority of the Church and its pastors, as absolutely as it may be asserted, is limited. That limitation is the word of God. We must remember that the one who is making these sweeping claims of authority for the Church is also the one who broke with the established Church of his day. He could do this only because he came to acknowledge an authority higher than the Church and one which countered the Church of his day. Furthermore, we must bear in mind Calvin's definition of the Church which contains within it the limitation. "Hence the visible Church rises conspicuous to our view. For wherever we find the word of God purely preached and heard, and the sacraments administered according to the institution of Christ, there, it is not to be doubted, is a Church of God."[30] This is a limitation at every point when one turns to Calvin's discussion of the sacraments and sees that they are determined by the word of God and differ in no essential point from it.

> If we grant . . . that the Church cannot err in things essential to salvation, our meaning is, that its security from error is owing to its renouncing all its own wisdom, and submitting itself to the Holy Spirit, to be taught by means of the word of God (*a Spiritu sancto docere se per verbum Dei, patitur*). This, then is the difference between us [Calvin and the Romans]. They ascribe to the Church an authority independent of the word; we maintain it to be annexed to the word, and inseparable from it (*nos autem volumus verbo annexam, nec ab eo separare patimur*).[31]

The authority granted to the Church and its pastors is not one granted to the institution as such and not at all to the persons of the ministers, but rather "to the ministry over which they were appointed, or, to speak more correctly, to the word, the ministration of which was committed to them."[32] Neither the Church nor its ministers can frame any new doctrine which has been conceived in their own minds. They are bound to deliver nothing other than the doctrine which has been delivered to them.[33]

The reason, again, for this careful delimitation must be clear. Were the situation otherwise we would be in the position of depending on an authority that is human and thus frail. "How will the impious ridicule our faith, and all men call it in question, if it be understood to possess only a precarious authority (*precariam authoritatem*) depending on the favour of men?"[34] "All persons of sound judgment perceive how exceedingly dangerous it would be if so much power were once granted to any man."[35] Only the Bible itself, as an authority, escapes this dilemma.

> Between the apostles and their successors, however, there is, as I have stated, this difference—that the apostles were the

certain and authentic amanuenses of the Holy Spirit (*certe et authentici Spiritus sancti amanuenses*), and therefore their writings are to be received as the oracles of God (*pro Dei oraculis*); but succeeding ministers have no other office than to teach what is revealed and recorded in the sacred Scriptures (*ut docent quod sacris Scripturis proditum est ac consignatum*).[36]

This statement may legitimately be considered as a summary of Calvin's view of all claims to authority other than the word. They must all be limited—some more, some less—because not one of them can be productive of that certainty required in our knowledge of God and man. Calvin had to hold on to the Bible, and although, after the foregoing discussion, one cannot say that he held on to the Bible alone, one can assert that he put the Bible above every other claim to authority in a determinative way, conceiving it to be in a qualitatively different class. His ambition, therefore, was to be one thing: a biblical theologian, *par excellence*.

The Practice of the Biblical Theologian

Calvin's practical pursuit of the biblical principle is more impressive than the predictable consistency with which he handled other claims to authority. One of the most stunning features of his writings is his amazing command of the Bible. The commentaries are written with a meticulous care which brings to bear on any passage not only a thorough knowledge of the book on which he is commenting but also what he may consider to be relevant passages from any other portion of the scriptures. In the *Institutes* he quotes profusely from the Bible, and his references are rarely systematic. They are taken from here, there, and yon, an indication that the writer has an incredible knowledge of his authority.

It is true that Calvin is prone to quote some parts of the Bible more than others. He refers, in the *Institutes*, only once to the Song of Solomon,[37] and that instance is neither clear nor important.* Calvin never quoted from Esther and one or two other

---

* It should be noted, however, that Calvin would have nothing of anyone trying to slight the importance of the Song of Solomon. It was because

books. On the other hand, Calvin quotes most often from the letters of Paul. It may even be said that he refers more abundantly to what we now believe are the genuine Pauline epistles, but he does not neglect the pastoral epistles, using them thoroughly in his discussion of Church order. He makes profuse use of the Psalms and is drawn again and again to the Gospel according to John and I John. Despite the fact that Calvin showed some preferences in his scripture references, the fact remains that he quoted from practically all parts with the same assumption of authority in all cases. It may also be noted that, unlike Luther, in his exegetical work Calvin moved from one book to another, never lecturing on the same book twice. Ostensibly, if he had lived long enough he would have produced a set of commentaries on the whole Bible.

In the *Institutes* Calvin's pursuit of the biblical principle can be seen most clearly in the fact that he depends on the Bible for the themes around which he has organized his instruction. This is his stated purpose in the Preface.* But the full weight of this intention is not felt until one has read through the *Institutes* and has seen the relentless force with which Calvin has carried out his intention.

One of the most lucid examples of this practice is found in Calvin's discussion of the Christian life in Book III. In this discussion he lays bare his mind, explicitly stating his methodology. He begins by announcing that he wants to draw up a rule for the reformation of life based upon scripture.[38] He makes it clear that the outline and the structure are his, whereas the illustrations and support for the various points are drawn from scripture. He justifies this method in the following way: "The Spirit, whose teaching is void of affectation, has not so exactly or perpetually observed a methodical plan; which, nevertheless, by using it in some places, he sufficiently indicates ought not to be neglected by us."[39] Even the arrangement of the biblical material in a systematic order,

---

Castellio, during his examination before the Compagnie Vénérable, had expressed doubts about the inspiration of this book that his application for admission to the pastorate was denied. See Williston Walker, *John Calvin*, pp. 288–91.

* See p. 22.

although the arrangement itself is nonbiblical, is justified by the Bible. The last thing Calvin wants to do is to create what might justifiably be called John Calvin's system. A system of that nature would then be no more authoritative than any of the other claims to authority, and exhorting men to accept it would be as weak as Apollo claiming that men should worship according to the laws of their own countries or cities—in short, it would be accepting something on the authority of men, and that is like building a house on the sand.*

The biblical material as the source for the themes discussed in the *Institutes* can be seen throughout that work. The discussion on natural theology is hardly more than Calvin's sustained exegesis of Rom. 1, and the contention that men *can* know God through the creation and the conscience is supported by passages such as Paul's speech on Mars Hill.[40] Even such a theme as the knowledge of one's own meanness, since it is dependent on a comparison with the divine majesty, is thoroughly documented with biblical evidence.[41] Calvin would furthermore maintain that he himself was not in the least original in joining word and Spirit as the norm of authority. Isaiah has done this, he points out, long ago.[42]

Occasionally what may not be seen in the *Institutes* is made clear in the commentaries. Calvin, of course, makes a great deal of the predictions of Christ in the Old Testament. It is true that this was common in Calvin's day, and the Genevan Reformer was much less vociferous in this respect than was the Wittenberger. But Calvin makes it clear in his commentary on John that this view of the Old Testament is justified not only by the many places in the New Testament which reflect the Old Testament, but also by Christ himself.[43] It may safely be said that at not one point in the *Institutes* does Calvin discuss a subject which is not explicitly derived, either there or in some other work of the author, from Holy Scripture.

The claim of reason as an authority was discussed above, where it was pointed out that, consistent with the biblical principle, Calvin positively subordinated human reason to the Bible. In reading the *Institutes* one gets the further impression that Calvin would

* See pp. 11–12.

define good reason as that which comes to a conclusion consonant with the scriptures. It has been noted that Calvin seldom admitted that anything in the Christian faith is irrational. Consequently there are many points where Calvin presents as clear logic what can at best be called curious reasoning.

This appears in two forms in the *Institutes*. It may be curious reasoning which subsequently proves to be nothing more than Calvin's own paraphrase of scripture, or it may be the author's attempt to justify rationally seemingly incongruous statements of scripture previously noted. A curiosity of the first variety occurs in his discussion of the knowledge of God in creation, a place where one would expect him to be operating, at least for the moment, without a dependence on scripture. The range of knowledge which Calvin claims is available to all men through nature is wider than that which is argued by some confessed natural theologians. It is his reasoning for rewards and punishments after death that is most curious. In this discussion Calvin argues for the knowledge of rewards and punishments both in the here and now and in the hereafter. The first case is made by calling attention to the well-being of the pious and the suffering of the wicked. The exceptions to this rule are the foundation of his argument for the same thing in the hereafter.

> Nor should it perplex or eclipse his perpetual rule of righteousness, that he frequently permits the wicked and guilty for a time to exult in impunity; but suffers good men to be undeservedly harassed with much adversity, and even to be oppressed by the iniquitous malice of the ungodly. We ought rather to make a very different reflection; that, when he clearly manifests his wrath in the punishment of one sin, he hates all sins; and that, since he now passes by many sins unpunished, there will be a judgment hereafter, till which the punishment is deferred.[44]

This is odd logic, to be sure, but the point is that it was suggested to him by certain passages in the Psalms, a fact made clear in the succeeding paragraph.[45]

In the discussion of the differences and similarities between the Old and New Testaments there is a glaring inconsistency in reasoning which we may safely assume would not have bothered

Calvin had it been pointed out to him. Indeed, he may well have been aware of it. In the chapter on similarities he is eloquent on the miseries of Abraham, Isaac, and Jacob as conclusive evidence that they had a higher hope than terrestrial blessings. He interprets Jacob's crafty contrivances as an "eminent example of nothing but extreme infelicity."[46] But Jacob was willing to endure all of this because he had his eyes set on eternal felicity. As one reads this section, one has the impression that Calvin is resorting to a fallacious argument and standing on it as a good one. It turns out, however, that he argues that way only because it is his understanding of Hebrews 11.[47] In the next chapter, however, Calvin has a good deal to say about the earthly felicity of these same fathers. Here this is also put forth as rather conclusive evidence that they looked forward to a celestial inheritance; only here it is necessary to look on these blessings as figures, or, to use Calvin's favorite metaphor, a mirror. "In the earthly possession which they enjoyed, they contemplated, as in a mirror, the future inheritance which they believed to be prepared for them in heaven."[48] To substantiate this interpretation he cites Paul in the fourth chapter of Galatians as well as Psalms.[49] On the one hand, his reading of the evidence is bad; on the other hand, he is inconsistent in the sense of drawing one conclusion from opposing readings of the same data. But in both instances he is standing firmly on the scripture.

The practice of giving a rationale for apparent conflicts within the Bible is best seen in his treatment of the problem of evil and in the discussions on providence and human responsibility. The latter discussion begins with the major premise, founded on scripture, that God is the ultimate cause of all things. The proper human response to this is not to take one's ease, but rather to be active. If God has given remedies for an ill, one should use them, and he is enjoined by God to do so. If this does not make good sense to a man, then he should heed Calvin's advice: "Examine whether your reasoning agrees with the order of the Divine providence."[50] The implication is that if it does not, then there is something wrong with your reason. What about men who do wickedly? Is this due to the divine causality? Calvin explains that one who does wrong is not complying with the divine will. After that, however, he adds that God can use human wickedness to subserve his will or to execute his judgments.[51]

When he discusses the problem of evil in Book II he makes use of multiple causality to solve a similar incongruity. The solution may also be applied to the former problem. Here he deals specifically with the suffering of Job, and at first sight the explanation seems to be, by intent at least, a rather subtle philosophical analysis. Calvin poses the problem lucidly: "How can we refer the same action to God, to Satan, and to man, as being each the author of it, without either excusing Satan by associating him with God, or making God the author of evil?"[52] The problem, he suggests, can be averted if we consider the end and the manner by which the end was effected. God's design was to try Job's patience, that of Satan was to drive him to despair, and that of the Chaldeans was to enrich themselves. The manner involved is, in the case of God, to permit Satan to afflict Job and the Chaldeans to be impelled by Satan. In the case of the devil, it was to instigate the minds of the Chaldeans to commit the crime, and in the case of the Chaldeans, it was to rush headlong into their destiny, thereby overwhelming themselves with guilt.

> Satan therefore is properly said to work in the reprobate, in whom he exercises his dominion; that is, the kingdom of iniquity. God also is said to work in a way proper to himself, because Satan, being the instrument of his wrath, turns himself hither and thither at his appointment and command, to execute his righteous judgments. . . . We see, then, that the same action is without absurdity ascribed to God, to Satan, and to man; but the variety in the end and in the manner, causes the righteousness of God to shine without the least blemish, and the iniquity of Satan and of man to betray itself to its own disgrace.[53]

In the succeeding paragraphs Calvin shows his hand more clearly. The entire explanation was simply his way of putting various scripture passages together and maintaining the truth of all of them. His summary comment is, "I think we are in no danger, if we simply maintain what the Scripture delivers."[54]

For a long time scholars have sought to find the key doctrine in Calvin's *Institutes*. Suggestions have run from the doctrine of election to the more broad suggestion of the sovereignty of God to the most general and consequently the most safe and consequently, perhaps, the least significant contention (in the sense that this key might be applied to many Christian theologians) that Christ is the key to the system. It is doubtful if the problem will ever be solved in such a way that scholars will concur in the solution.

This is somewhat surprising inasmuch as this is not a problem with most theologians. The very fact that scholars have not been able to agree on the key doctrine ought to suggest the possibility that Calvin had no one central dogma from which all the others were derived. But there is a more conclusive reason for considering this as a possibility: that is the intention of the author himself. He desired to be one thing, a biblical theologian. He considered it his task in the *Institutes* to arrange the mass of biblical material into a systematic order, but he did not consider it his task to derive a system of dogma from one overarching doctrine. He accomplished his task, faithful to the last to his guiding maxim. He did bring order out of the chaos, but this did not consist in putting one biblical theme above another, but rather in setting all the major themes of the Bible side by side. It was precisely this which he set out to do in the first place.

It has been the purpose of this chapter to call attention to the fact that the main thing one must see in Calvin is the biblical principle put into application with overwhelming persistence. Insofar as any attempt to point to a core doctrine obscures this, it draws the student's mind away from what must be understood as Calvin's own explicit "solution" to the "enigma" of his theology.

"He who knows how to use the Scriptures properly, is in want of nothing for salvation, or for a holy life."[55]

The Implicit Distinction
in Calvin's Use of
His Principle of Authority

Important as it is to take notice of Calvin's statement of authority, the rationale behind it, and to understand the certainty issuing from this authority, there is something more important to the contemporary appreciation of his theology. And although the student of Calvin should recognize the determinative quality of the biblical principle throughout the Reformer's work, this is only the first stage in comprehending his use of the Bible as the sole authority for the Christian faith.

In other words, it is not enough to discover *what* was Calvin's principle of authority and how he felt about it. Nor is it sufficient to see *that* he applied it in a general way with apparently unerring consistency. We must go on to ask *how* he applied it. This question implies a number of questions of a different character from those which have been asked up to now. Up to this point we have been discussing basic conceptions and in a general way the faithfulness with which they were used. As a foundation for the full understanding of Calvin's doctrine of the authority of scripture this is indispensable, but now we must move on to ask more pointed questions and to speak with more detail and more preciseness.

We have seen that Calvin's exposition of the Christian faith centers around the concept of knowledge.* "True and substantial wisdom," he notes at the beginning of the *Institutes*, "principally consists of two parts, the knowledge of God, and the knowledge

* See p. 9.

of ourselves (*Dei cognitione et nostri*)."[1] Throughout his work it is knowledge that Calvin is seeking to transmit to his readers, and his violent polemic against the Roman Catholic conception of implicit faith is explained by the fact that implicit faith means faith without knowledge.

The very use of this category by Calvin ought to give the modern interpreter pause. Certainly, in contemporary theological and philosophical discussions there is no single theory of knowledge on which there is wide agreement, and the term itself has a variety of meanings, with the result that the word can be understood in its use by a particular thinker only after careful study. But even if present-day thinkers were agreed on the meaning and use of the word, there would be a danger in assuming that John Calvin operated with the same meaning and use. We must, therefore, pose a number of questions to our author on his understanding and use of the category. We must ask how one comes to know and what is the character of this knowing. We must inquire after the content of the knowledge about which he speaks, and it will also be instructive to note what Calvin considers to be the proper human response to this knowledge. When we do this it will be seen that Calvin operates with two distinct epistemologies, which, although they cannot be radically separated from one another, do submit to study in isolation from one another by virtue of the fact that they supply different answers to the questions suggested above. On the one hand, there is one epistemology for faith, and on the other hand, there is another for what may be called the wider knowledge, or, to use Calvin's words, for anything "that has proceeded from God's sacred mouth." Both of these epistemologies are derived from the same statement of authority: the correlation of word and Spirit.

The questions which we will pose to Calvin on his use of the term knowledge constitute, of course, the heart of the problem involved in fully understanding his use of the principle of authority. But we will find that the distinction uncovered in that study holds true for other areas of discussion; for example, the problem of Calvin's certainty. We noted his craving for certainty, and one of the most impressive facts about Calvin's writings is the absolute certainty reflected by the author at every point. When we investigate this certainty and probe for its foundations and meaning we will find that, although it is always derived from the one principle of authority (the correlation of word and Spirit), there is a perceptible distinction depending on whether the object of the certainty is the knowledge of faith or what we mean by the wider knowledge.

Since it is the purpose of this essay to understand Calvin's principle of authority, we should submit the elements of the authoritative compound to a close scrutiny. We must probe his understanding of the word and the Spirit. This will involve a study of Calvin's use of the scriptures. In pursuit of this study we will want to analyze his exegetical tools and methods. We will also want to examine the exegesis itself at several points. In connection with this it will be necessary to enter the already filled arena in which the battle over Calvin's theory of inspiration is being fought. Again, we will find that there is a perceptible distinction in Calvin's use of the Bible and perhaps a double theory of inspiration consonant with the distinction previously noted. In the discussion of the Holy Spirit we will find that the Holy Spirit works one way in producing faith and in a distinctly different way in conveying the wider knowledge.

In all these discussions it will be necessary to assess the fitness of the principle of authority as well as to call attention to some of the problems Calvin faces in using his authority and the ways in which he meets and solves these problems.

The distinction has been referred to as "implicit" in Calvin's writings. That is not entirely correct. Actually Calvin makes it quite clear that not everything in the Bible is to be read on the same level of importance. As a matter of fact, a surprisingly large number of matters in the Bible are inconsequential. In the commentary on the Gospel according to John, for example, Calvin points out that he prefers the indicative translation of the ambiguous second person plural, present tense of the verb "to know," but he adds that he has no objection if anyone wants to read it as an imperative. And immediately after that he writes that he understands what is translated "before you" in terms of rank rather

than time. But again this is only a preference.[2] In the exegesis
of the healing of the blind man in which Jesus made use of clay,
Calvin flatly rejects allegory, but then he gives two possible interpretations and only indicates at the end which one he person-
ally prefers.[3] Furthermore, it is not entirely unusual to find a
statement such as this: "On that point, however, I will not enter
into a debate with any person; only I wish to remind the reader,
that he ought to adopt that view which appears to him to derive
greater probability from the context."[4] This openness is ordinarily
exhibited only on points of translation and exegesis where the
meaning of the passage under consideration will not be materially
affected regardless of the way one understands it. There are times,
however, when the only conceivable reason for the latitude is the
conviction of the author that the passage is not important. At any
rate the point stands, and it is somewhat enlightening to hear one
of Calvin's persuasion say, "It doesn't matter."

Such an attitude is not actually surprising. It is questionable
if it would be humanly possible in practice to maintain that every
word of the text is of crucial importance. If it were done, the
result would most certainly be a rather grotesque and conglomer-
ated mass. But Calvin admits to a distinction in importance even
beyond this predictable one. It may be seen in his remarks which
preface the commentary on the Gospel of John.

> But as the bare history (*nuda historia*) would not be
> enough, and, indeed, would be of no advantage for salvation,
> the Evangelists do not merely relate that Christ was born, and
> that he died and vanquished death, but also explain for what
> purpose (*in quem finem*) he was born, and died, and rose
> again, and what benefit we derive from those events (*quis inde
> ad nos redeat fructus*).[5]

Here we see that there is an acknowledgement that not everything
in the Bible is of the same character. Calvin distinguishes between
nuda historia and *historia salutis*, the history of salvation (perhaps
even *Heilsgeschichte*). It is important to note that the Bible does
not have one kind of history (*historia salutis*) rather than the
other (*nuda historia*). Both kinds of history are related in the
Bible. It might be deduced that Calvin in the above passage is

merely distinguishing between history and interpretation and calling attention to the fact that the history by itself is of no avail unless we are led to the meaning of the history. Of course, that is the case, but elsewhere Calvin makes a similar distinction in relation to the *importance* of various parts of the scriptures.

This crucial distinction appears repeatedly in the chapter on faith in the *Institutes*.[6] To recognize the position of this acknowledgement in the *Institutes* is of the utmost importance. It presents the student with an invaluable clue to the understanding of Calvin's theology. If the distinction is significant, then the point at which it occurs may well be the axis around which the entire work revolves. That is, I think, the case. Although it cannot be said that Calvin's doctrine of faith is that overarching doctrine from which all others are derived, it can be said that it is the high point of the *Institutes* and that doctrine with which Calvin struggles to relate all other doctrines.

The distinction is most certainly clear and forthright. It appears first in the seventh paragraph of the chapter on faith, where those parts of the Bible which extol God's mercy are distinguished from the rest of the Bible as the object of faith. The paragraph begins, "But as the human heart is not excited (*erigitur*) to faith by every word of God (*ad vocem Dei quamlibet*), we must further inquire what part of the word it is, with which faith is particularly concerned (*quid proprie fides in verbo respiciat*)."[7] Then, after citing a couple of examples of God's wrath from the Old Testament—examples which would shake faith rather than establish it—he continues with a guarding statement: "We do not deny that it is the office of faith to subscribe to the truth of God (*veritate Dei subscribere*), whatever be the time, the nature, or the manner of his communications; but our present inquiry is only, what faith finds in the Divine word (*quid in verbo Domini reperiat fides*), upon which to rest its dependence and confidence."[8] But even in declaring the necessity of the whole, Calvin makes it clear that one part particularly has to do with the establishment of faith. In making this declaration he stood closer than at any other point to his counterpart in Germany.

A little later in the same chapter Calvin returns to this distinc-

tion, this time in the context of an examination of the double
meaning of the word "faith."

> We must also remember the ambiguous signification of
> the word *faith*; for frequently faith signifies the sound doc-
> trine of piety. . . . On the contrary, it is sometimes restricted
> to a particular object. . . . And we have lately shown, that
> Paul uses faith for the gift of miracles; which is possessed by
> those who are neither regenerated by the Spirit of God, nor
> serious worshippers of him. In another place, also, he uses it
> to denote the instruction by which we are edified in the faith
> (*Alibi etiam fidem ponit pro doctrina qua in fide instituimur*).
> . . . In these forms of expression, however, there is an evident
> analogy. But our present inquiry is, what is that faith by which
> the children of God are distinguished from unbelievers, by
> which we invoke God as our Father, by which we pass from
> death to life, and by which Christ, our eternal life and salva-
> tion, dwells in us?[9]

The way Calvin puts the first four uses of "faith" in the Bible
together and separates the fifth is similar to the distinction sometimes made by theologians between faith and belief. Although
that present-day distinction constitutes a rather artificial and
brittle use of the words, it is occasionally useful. In this instance
it is helpful in leading the student of Calvin to recognize the author's qualitative differentiation between instruction which involves the credibility of the entire Bible and faith proper which
fastens on the promises of God's grace.

Still later Calvin comes forth with another guarding statement,
which, like the one noted above, reveals that he distinguishes even
though he does not under any circumstance reject.

> We make the foundation of faith to be the gratuitous prom-
> ise (*gratuitam promissionem*); for on that faith properly rests
> (*in ipso proprie fides consistat*). For although faith admits
> the veracity of God in all things (*Deum per omnia veracem
> esse statuat*), whether he command or prohibit, whether he
> promise or threaten; though it obediently (*obedienter*) re-
> ceives his injunctions, carefully observes his prohibitions, and
> attends to his threatenings,—yet with the promise it properly
> begins, on that it stands, and in that it ends (*proprie tamen a
> promissione incipit, in ipsa constat, in ipsam desinit*).[10]

This is the most instructive statement we have yet observed. It indicates the full sweep of the biblical material which is not *in a peculiar way* central to the very heart of the Christian gospel. Indeed, that range of material, whatever one's attitude toward it may be, cannot make one a Christian. "If any man believe the justice of the Divine commands and the truth of the Divine threatenings, must he therefore be called a believer? By no means. Therefore faith can have no stability, unless it be placed on the Divine mercy (*Firmus ergo fidei status non erit, nisi in Dei misericordia sistatur*)."[11]

It would be improper to conclude from the above discussion that Calvin considered one part of the scripture (that dealing especially with the promises of divine mercy) of greater importance than the rest. For one thing, that has not been the point of the discussion. The point of the discussion has been rather that Calvin did make a distinction in the mass of the biblical material beyond what would have to be expected of any exegete. It is not essential that one part be thought of as higher than another, but it is important to note in this distinction that the object of the one body of material is faith.

If we are to avoid a misunderstanding of our author's position, we must see his discussion in the wider context of the chapter on faith as well as in his theology as a whole. It has been noted that occasionally in making the distinction Calvin includes a guarding statement. It may be added that before he draws the distinction for the first time he makes a basic declaration which clearly indicates the unity which underlies the distinction. This occurs when he asserts that faith is a knowledge of the divine will toward us.

For the apprehension of faith is not confined to our knowing that there is a God, but chiefly consists in our understanding (*intelligamus*) what is his disposition towards us (*qua sit erga nos voluntate*). For it is not of so much importance to us to know what he is in himself (*scire quis in se sit*), as what he is willing to be to us (*sed qualis esse nobis velit*). We find, therefore, that faith is a knowledge of the will of God respecting us, received from his word (*divinae erga nos voluntatis notitiam ex eius verbo perceptam*). And the foundation of this is a previous persuasion of the divine veracity (*praesumpta de*

veritate Dei persuasio); any doubt of which being entertained
in the mind, the authority of the word will be dubious and
weak, or rather it will be of no authority at all (*vel potius
nullius authoritatis erit verbum*). Nor is it sufficient to believe
that the veracity of God is incapable of deception or falsehood,
unless you also admit, as beyond all doubt, that whatever proceeds from him is sacred and inviolable truth.*

It is proper to say that Calvin makes a distinction within the mass
of the biblical material, but not at all if we understand by that
term a separation of any kind. Faith may fasten on the divine
promises as distinguished from the rest of the Bible, but faith in
the divine promises depends in turn on a certain persuasion of the
truthfulness of God—and this is a persuasion not only that the
promises are true but also of the veracity of God in all things,
meaning by that the entire Bible.

If the foundation of faith is the veracity of God in all things,
then the issue of it also goes far beyond what we have seen to be
faith's particular object. Faith is trust in the divine mercy, but it
never remains that narrow. Beginning there it blossoms out into
a full knowledge—a knowledge as full as the word of God. In
commenting on the conversion of the jailer by Paul and Silas in
Acts 16, Calvin notes that it was sufficient for the jailer to believe
in Christ in order to be saved, but it was also necessary that Paul
and Silas preach to him because faith must have knowledge. This
causes the writer to move into a characteristic emphasis on preaching and doctrine. If these are omitted there will soon be no faith at
all because faith cannot be vague.[12]

It is appropriate to ask if Calvin attributed any significance
to this distinction, and such a question demands a candid reply.
Insofar as Calvin himself suggests it, along with the value judgments we have already observed, the question may be answered in
the affirmative. On the other hand, however, he certainly did not
notice the extent of its importance. The suggestions that Calvin
operates with two distinct theories of knowledge, two ways of
using the Bible and of understanding its inspiration and two

* III. ii. 6 (O.S. IV. 15.6–18). Calvin makes essentially the same
point in the commentary on John 4:22 (C.O. 47.87–88).

separable—perhaps disparate—vocabularies about the work of the Holy Spirit, are interpretations; Calvin himself does not explicitly pursue the distinction beyond what has already been noted. As a sixteenth-century figure, most likely it never occurred to him. For the purpose of understanding our theologian, however, it will be necessary to search his entire work with this distinction in mind, and critical questions will be more precise if one does not lose sight of it. In the chapters that follow, we will probe Calvin's understanding of knowledge and his principle of authority from a variety of angles in order to come to a more complete understanding of his theology. In doing this it will be seen that the distinction made by Calvin himself is of help in understanding and evaluating his correlation of word and Spirit as the final authority in the Christian faith.

PART II

Spirit

The Work of the Spirit
in the Writers of the Bible

There has never been any doubt about the general boundaries of the principle of authority in Calvin's theology. Clearly enough, it is the correlation of word and Spirit. As one seeks a more precise understanding of the principle, however, he readily perceives several areas of investigation under each pole of the correlation. We will ask first about the work of the Spirit, after which we will inquire into Calvin's understanding of the word. The first will require an investigation of the work of the Spirit in the writers of the Bible and in believers, the latter of which includes the Church and her leaders as well as lay Christians. The other will take us into the question of knowledge, its content and character as well as the response of the believer to it, and into a review of Calvin's exegetical work as it bears on an understanding of authority.

To speak of the work of the Spirit in the writers of the Bible is to embark on a discussion of the inspiration of the scriptures. This has been a much worked-over area in Calvin scholarship, and it most likely will continue to be worked over inasmuch as the major scholars are generally in disagreement with one another. The appetite of the authorities is further whetted by the curious fact that although this is a topic of central importance Calvin nowhere develops an independent discussion of it. In the present day, those who are more or less of the Barthian school tend to minimize the evidence in Calvin for a literal dictation theory of inspiration for the purpose of claiming that Calvin held the scripture to be a real witness to the revelation rather than the revelation itself.[1] On the other hand, there are some who cannot dispense with the data supporting the other view and who therefore claim that Calvin held more or less to a dictation theory or who point back to the validity of Warfield's conclusion: "It is not unfair to urge, however, . . . that what Calvin has in mind, is, not to insist that the mode of inspiration was dictation, but that the result of inspiration is as if it were by dictation, viz., the production of a pure word of God free from all human admixtures."[2]

Calvin and the "Dictation" Theory

In his essay dealing with biblical authority in the Continental Reformation Brian A. Gerrish calls attention to the quite obvious, but often overlooked, fact that the reformers lived in a time when the dictation theory of inspiration went unchallenged in principle.[3] Recognizing this, one should expect from Calvin adherence to the dictation theory, especially when one considers that he did not explicitly develop a theory to the contrary. Certainly as one reads Calvin and notes his language about the work of the Spirit in the writers of the Bible, his first impulse is to conclude that without doubt Calvin believed the human writers to be an almost negligible element in the production of the scriptures.

It is as easy—one should probably say easier—for Calvin to speak of the scriptures as the writings of the Spirit as to think of them as the product of the men who actually moved the pens. His writings are liberally sprinkled—one should probably say filled —with such statements as, "The Spirit speaks in the Scriptures."[4] "The Spirit has expressly predicted by the mouth of Paul,"[5] "the Spirit is accustomed to speak,"[6] "the Spirit declares there,"[7] "we must keep in mind the design of the Holy Spirit."[8] Indeed, we might almost say that it was Calvin's intent to speak in this way at every point, for he occasionally corrects himself after having referred to the human writer by name, as when he writes, "This order and connection did David observe, or rather the Spirit of God, who meant by the mouth of David to instruct the whole Church."[9] That this is the case we must suspect even more by virtue of the fact that not once does Calvin say in effect, "These are the words of David (or whoever), not of the Holy Spirit."

He comes close to it on rare occasions. One such occurs in his commentary on Ezekiel, where Calvin, with his quite amazing understanding of Hebrew and his humanistic eye for style, makes observations on the language of the prophet.

> Ezekiel is verbose in this narration. But in the beginning of the book we said, that because the teacher was sent to men very slow and stupid, he therefore used a rough style. We added also, that he had acquired it partly from the custom of the region in which he dwelt. For the people declined by degrees from the polish of their language, and hence it happens that the Prophet's diction is not quite pure, but is intermixed with something foreign.[10]

It is interesting, however, that although Calvin speaks of Ezekiel's verbosity and diction, he gives himself an out, if one were called for, by stating that the people to whom the prophet addressed himself were such that they demanded this particular style. It may be added that Calvin in his discussion of the rational proofs for the belief in scripture in the *Institutes* declares one reason to be that the Spirit was able to speak in the most lofty as well as in the most mean style.[11]

Sometimes Calvin takes up in a critical way more serious matters than style. One of the most astounding instances of this is in his comments on Psalm 39. "I admit, that he [David] speaks in a becoming manner, in acknowledging that there is no hope of his being restored to health, until God cease to manifest his displeasure: but he errs in this, that he asks a respite, just that he may have time to die."[12] This is serious because it admits a human error in the text. But Calvin will not leave the matter with no positive word. "We might, indeed, regard the prayer as allowable, by understanding it in this sense: Lord, as it will not be possible for me to endure thy stroke any longer, but I must, indeed, miserably perish, if thou continuest to afflict me severely, at least grant me relief for a little season, that in calmness and peace I may commit my soul into thy hands."[13] With that meaning as the genuine one Calvin could say that the words have been prompted by the Spirit. However, he realizes that although this is a possible meaning, the words of the Psalmist are somewhat strained by it. So he adds,

But we may easily infer, from the language which he employs, that his mind was so affected with the bitterness of his grief that he could not present a prayer pure and well seasoned with the sweetness of faith; for he says, *before I depart, and be no more*: a form of speech which indicates the feeling almost of despair. . . . It is obvious, therefore, that, although David endeavoured carefully to restrain the desires of the flesh, yet these occasioned him so much disquietude and trouble, that they forced him to exceed the proper limits in his grief.[14]

The reader of Calvin may legitimately ask where the dictation of the Holy Spirit is in this passage. However, Calvin did not disclaim the Spirit's authorship. If he had been pressed on this point he had an answer available in a principle worked out mainly in his discussion of the problem of evil but equally applicable here, especially since he saw a possible interpretation that would be acceptable. The reference is to multiple causation. He could have said (it is not for us to say whether he would have) that although David's words were unbecoming, the Spirit, speaking through David and using David's excess, intended something entirely acceptable—indeed, something necessary to be known.

Those who seek to minimize Calvin's literalism are most interested in setting his position over against the dictation theory of present-day "fundamentalists." To be sure, it is a question if Calvin meant by dictation precisely the same thing that is currently understood by that term. Assuredly the flavor of Calvin's writings differs from that of some of the most notable arch-conservatives on the American scene.* However, whether Calvin held to a

---

* Note particularly the numerous writings of Carl F. H. Henry and Edward John Carnell, who are peculiarly American, and Cornelius Van Til, who combines Dutch Reformed conservatism with the spirit of American fundamentalism. These men are not always in agreement with one another, but they share a rationalistic style, putting great stock in the power of their logic. In this they differ somewhat from John Calvin, and they also indicate their dependence on the earlier Calvin scholar, Warfield, who, although he made many lasting contributions to Calvin research, generally made too much of Calvin's rationalism. Compare his appraisal of the *indicia* (the rational proofs for the belief in scripture) in *Calvin and Calvinism*, pp. 84ff.

The major works of these conservatives are listed in the Bibliography.

"dictation theory" is not debatable. He did. He is constantly speaking of the work of the biblical writers as having been "dictated" by the Holy Spirit or by Christ. The prayers which are found in the Bible are spoken of in this vein. "Whoever was the penman of the Psalm, the Holy Spirit seems, by his mouth, to have dictated a common form of prayer for the Church in her afflictions (*videtur spiritus per os eius communem precande formam per afflicta ecclesia dictasse*)."[15] "In these words the Holy Ghost dictates to us a form of prayer (*in his verbis dictari nobis a spiritu sancto precandi formam*."[16] His comment at the end of his exposition of the Lord's Prayer can only be taken as all-inclusive: "The Scriptures contain many prayers, expressed in words very different from this, yet written by the same Spirit (*eodem tamen Spiritu conscriptae*), and very profitable for our use."[17]

It is not only of prayers but of everything that Calvin uses this kind of language. "The ancient prophecies," he writes, "were dictated by Christ (*a Christo dictatas*)."[18] "Daniel did not speak from his own discretion, but whatever he uttered was dictated by the Holy Spirit (*Danielem non loquutum esse ex proprio sensu, sed dictatam fuisse a spiritu sancto quidquid protulit*)."[19] Of course, Moses in commending his own continuance had no intention of boasting. Rather "the Holy Spirit dictated (*dictavit spiritus*) what would be useful to us, and, as it were, suggested it to his mouth (*in os illius suggessit*), that what he did and suffered might be an example for ever."[20] In short, Calvin could say of all the writers of the canonical books that they were "the certain and authentic amanuenses of the Holy Spirit (*certi et authentici Spiritus sancti amanuenses*)."*

---

* IV. viii. 9 (O.S. V. 141.13–14). The canon, for Calvin, was limited to the 39 books of the Old Testament and the 27 books of the New. He evidently did not consider it at all necessary to discuss the extent of the canon. It should be remembered that although the Apocrypha was generally considered authoritative, Calvin did not set a precedent in rejecting it. Indeed, its authority was almost universally considered to be subsidiary, and it was not until the Council of Trent that it was declared by the Church to be a part of the canon.

Although Calvin has no separate discussion of the canon, he does explicitly include books such as James, II Peter, Jude, Revelation, and Song of Solomon, about which there may have been some questions. Further-

Doumergue[21] and numerous other authors claim that when Calvin speaks of the Holy Spirit "speaking through the mouths" of the writers and "dictating" to them and when he refers to the authors as the amanuenses of the Holy Spirit, his language must be understood as figurative. It is interesting that a conservative scholar like Warfield[22] admits that this is not an "unfair" reading of the sources. This argument is most frequently based on Calvin's numerous references to the scriptures as a "mirror."* In commenting on Jeremiah's prophecy Calvin writes, "Thus, as in a mirror, the Holy Spirit of God sets before us how great the madness of men is when Satan once takes possession of their hearts."[23] He can also speak of the Law as a mirror which shows us up for what we are, reflecting the spots and blemishes on our faces.[24] The most important statement in this regard is as follows: "The word itself, however it may be conveyed to us, is like a mirror, in which faith may behold God."[25] Peter Brunner makes clear the significance of this metaphor when he writes, "The mirror reflects an image that is quite clear, but the image reflected by the mirror is not the thing itself."[26]

There is some question, however, as to how much should be made of this metaphor in our understanding of Calvin's view of the scripture and the Spirit's work in its production. It was prob-

more, he occasionally refers to his exclusion of the books of the Apocrypha as a "right" [see III. xv. 4 (O.S. IV. 242.32–34)]. Or he might say that an apocryphal book is to be believed only if it can be interpreted in a way consonant with undoubted scripture [II. v. 18 (O.S. III. 318)], which is reminiscent of his appraisal of all subsidiary authorities. His most interesting reference to the Apocrypha has to do with the exclusion of Maccabees from the canon: "But why am I now contending to no purpose [in arguing about the interpretation of a passage there] as though the author himself did not sufficiently show what deference is due to him, when, at the conclusion, he begs pardon if he should have spoken any thing improperly? Certainly he who confesses that his writings need pardon, proclaims them not to be the oracles of the Holy Spirit" [III. v. 8 (O.S. IV. 141.1–5)]. It is instructive to compare this with Calvin's exegesis of II Cor. 7:8 (C.O. 50.88), where he forcefully disclaims that Paul's repentance of what he wrote in I Corinthians means that I Corinthians was written under a rash impulse. See below, p. 59.

* Doumergue, p. 73: *Il ne faut pas en effet s'en laisser imposer par les locutions: scribe, notaire, bouche de Dieu, etc. Ce sont des images, comme l'expression de "miroir."*

ably Calvin's most favorite metaphor, and he used it in relation
to all sorts of things. Creation is a mirror just like the Bible, and
"before the fall, the state of the world was a most fair and delight-
ful mirror of the divine favour and paternal indulgence towards
man."[27] The Church, also, is a mirror, and here not only for men
but also for angels in which "they behold the astonishing wisdom
of God displayed in a manner unknown to them before."[28] Man
is spoken of as a mirror of the divine glory,[29] and Calvin could
exalt Prince Christopher, Duke of Württemberg, using the mirror
metaphor: "I consider, therefore, that it is highly advantageous
to the whole Church, to hold out in you, as in a bright mirror, an
example which all may imitate."[30]

Keeping in mind Brunner's explanation of the meaning of the
term, Calvin's varied use of it becomes most perplexing when we
see his use of it for Christ. In one place, for example, Calvin
refers to Christ as the mirror of the grace of God,[31] whereas in
another place He is "the mirror in which it behoves us to contemplate our election."[32] The total complex of uses which Calvin
makes of this metaphor is rather astounding. To be sure, a mirror
gives one a reflection rather than that which it reflects; but, on
the one hand, those who make much of the Bible as a mirror in
Calvin would not want to say that men (certainly not a particular
man), creation, or even the Church can be a mirror in the same
sense; nor, on the other hand, would they want to say that the
scripture mirrors truth in precisely the same way that Christ does.
It is unthinkable that Calvin would have made the former associ-
ation, and questionable if he would have made the latter one.

The argument based on the metaphor of the mirror is not a
negligible one (Doumergue's work must be studied with respect),
but neither is it conclusive. What weight it can carry is probably
offset by quite explicit statements which can hardly be explained
in any but one way.

> If God, accommodating himself to the limited capacity of
> men, speaks in an humble and lowly style, this manner of
> teaching is despised as too simple; but if he rise to a higher
> style, with the view of giving greater authority to his Word,
> men, to excuse their ignorance, will pretend that it is too ob-

scure. As these two vices are very prevalent in the world, the Holy Spirit so tempers his style (*spiritus sanctus stylum ita temperat*) as that the sublimity of the truths which he teaches is not hidden even from those of the weakest capacity, provided they are of a submissive and teachable disposition, and bring with them an earnest desire to be instructed.[33]

Even the style of writing in the Bible is the work of the Holy Spirit. It is difficult to see how such language as this could be understood as "figurative."

It has also been contended that Calvin distinguished "the one Word and the words of Scripture, Jesus Christ the soul of the Bible and the extant written message which bears witness to Him."[34] Whether this is actually the case at any time remains to be seen; that it is not always or even predominantly the case can readily be seen.

> Not one of the prophets opened his mouth, therefore, without having first received the words from the Lord (*nisi Domino verba præeunte*). Hence their frequent use of these expressions; "The word of the Lord," "The burden of the Lord," "Thus saith the Lord," "The mouth of the Lord hath spoken;" and this was highly necessary; for Isaiah exclaimed, "I am a man of unclean lips;" (Isa. 6:5) and Jeremiah said, "Behold, I cannot speak, for I am a child." (Jer. 1:6) What could proceed from the pollution of the one, and the folly of the other, but impure and foolish speeches, if they had spoken their own words? But their lips were holy and pure, when they began to be the organs (*organa*) of the Holy Spirit.*

The German Calvin expert, Wilhelm Niesel, in trying to distinguish Calvin from the literalists, also claims that the Genevan put himself on record in opposition to the patchwork method of putting scripture verses together to make a point. "He [Calvin] expressly guards himself against exegesis which consists in the patching together of texts."[35] Niesel makes a footnote reference to the third paragraph in Calvin's chapter on the Trinity in Book I of the *Institutes*. One may say that Niesel missed the point in that paragraph. There Calvin is arguing that it is not necessary to bind

---

* IV. viii. 3 (O.S. IV. 135.22–30). This bears a striking similarity to the language of the fundamentalists.

oneself completely to the language of the scriptures in setting forth a doctrine. In this case, he argues, it is legitimate to use language not found in the Bible, so long as one is sure that what he says is substantiated in scripture. "If they call every word exotic, which cannot be found in the Scriptures in so many syllables, they impose on us a law which is very unreasonable, and which condemns all interpretation, but what is composed of detached texts of Scripture connected together."[36] It is not the connection of detached scripture passages to which Calvin objects here; rather it is limiting oneself exclusively to such a practice. The statement which follows hard upon the one just quoted clarifies Calvin's position considerably: "But if by exotic they mean that which is curiously contrived, and superstitiously defended, which tends to contention more than to edification, the use of which is either unseasonable or unprofitable, which offends pious ears with its harshness, and seduces persons from the simplicity of the Divine word, I most cordially embrace their modest opinion."[37]

Aside from the question of whether or not Calvin protected himself against the practice of patching together scripture verses, the fact is that on occasion he did patch. Let it suffice to call attention to the technique he used in proving the divinity of the Holy Spirit, which curiously enough comes in the same chapter to which Niesel referred. In one place Calvin connects I Corinthians 12:8 with Exodus 4:11. The one reads that the Holy Spirit "bestows wisdom and the faculty of speech," and in the other "the Lord declares to Moses, that this can only be done by himself."[38] The conclusion is obvious. The Holy Spirit is to be identified with God. He is therefore divine as God is divine. Calvin later adds this similar argument: "Indeed, while the Prophets invariably declare, that the words which they utter are those of the Lord of hosts, Christ and the Apostles refer them to the Holy Spirit; whence it follows, that he is the true Jehovah, who is the primary author of the prophecies."[39] This is not only the connection of rather detached texts; it also indicates a way of handling the scripture which puts a good deal of confidence in particular words.

Having made this clear, we may go on to point out that there may have been little or no distinction in Calvin's mind between the words of scripture and the doctrine. There are many contemporary theologians who hold quite strongly to the authority of the Bible in terms of doctrine who would not think of asserting that every word of scripture has been divinely inspired. Such men legitimately find many helpful statements in Calvin. On a number of occasions it seems that it is the doctrine about which Calvin is most concerned. As indicated in Chapter III,* Calvin can look on many words and their translation as being rather inconsequential, and when he speaks exclusively of doctrine in the argument prefacing his commentary on Joshua he is not out of character with himself. Although we may not be sure of the author, he writes there, "we are in no doubt as to the essential point—that the doctrine herein contained was dictated by the Holy Spirit for our use, and confers benefits of no ordinary kind on those who attentively peruse it."[40] It is also instructive to note here that Calvin refers to the doctrine as having been dictated. He either equated doctrine with the words or he, at least in this place, used it in a rather loose or figurative sense.

A conclusion on these alternatives may not be possible, but we may be sure that it was Calvin's concern to maintain that the whole of the scripture is true. If, in proclaiming this position, he occasionally refers to the words per se, then that is all the more evidence that Calvin could not separate the whole from its parts. "Whatever then is delivered in Scripture we ought to strive to learn; for it were a reproach offered to the Holy Spirit to think that he has taught anything which it does not concern us to know, let us also know, that whatever is taught us conduces to the advancement of religion."[41] It is unthinkable to Calvin that there could be an error anywhere in the text of scripture. "His word will ever be found free from every stain or defect,"[42] he declares. And in II Corinthians 7:8, when Paul indicates a certain remorse about the harsh words he had written in an earlier letter, Calvin focuses all his ingenuity as an exegete in order to explain that Paul did not disclaim what he had written.

* Pp. 39–40.

But what does he mean when he adds—though I did repent? For if we admit, that Paul had felt dissatisfied with
what he had written, there would follow an inconsistency of
no slight character—that the former Epistle had been written
under a rash impulse, rather than under the guidance of the
Spirit. I answer, that the word repent is used here in a loose
sense (*improprie*) for being grieved. For while he made the
Corinthians sad, he himself also participated in the grief, and
in a manner inflicted grief at the same time upon himself.[43]

In sum, "let us, therefore, set it down as certain and undoubted,
that whatever is from God is right and true, and that it is impossible for God not to be true in all his words (*in omnis verbis suis*),
just and right in all his actions."[44]

The point of the whole argument, then, is that the truth of God,
insofar as it can be known by man, is found only in the Bible.
"Since we are not favoured with daily oracles from heaven, and
since it is only in the Scriptures that the Lord hath been pleased
to preserve his truth in perpetual remembrance, it obtains the
same complete credit and authority with believers, when they are
satisfied of its divine origin, as if they heard the very words pronounced by God himself."[45]

The holy book is the work of the Holy Spirit. On this fundamental point Calvin bases his immutable conviction in the unity
of the scripture. "He [the Holy Spirit] is the author of the Scriptures: he cannot be mutable and inconsistent with himself. He
must therefore perpetually remain such as he has there discovered
himself to be."[46] On the basis of this belief in the authorship of
the Holy Spirit and the consequent unity of scripture, Calvin
considers it the task of every exegete to reconcile all apparent
divergencies in scripture. These can only be apparent; it is inconceivable that there should be actual divergencies. The Spirit
cannot be inconsistent with himself. So at the end of his discussion in the *Institutes* of the similarities and differences of the Old
and New Testaments, in which the point of the whole is that there
is no significant difference, the decisive point of his argument is
that the unity of the Testaments rests in their divine authorship.
He concludes, "God ought not therefore to be deemed mutable,

because he has accommodated different forms to different ages, as he knew would be suitable to each."[47] On the problem of the unity of the four gospels he has this to say: "He [God] therefore dictated to the Four Evangelists what they should write, in such a manner that, while each had his own part assigned him, the whole might be collected into one body; and it is our duty now to blend the Four by a mutual relation, so that we may permit ourselves to be taught by all of them, as by one mouth."*

Directly related to this understanding of the unity of scripture is the observation that Calvin's principle of the Bible as its own interpreter is based on the authorship of the Holy Spirit. If it is a recognized principle of contemporary exegesis that the obscure passages in a biblical writer are to be interpreted by the more clear statements of the same man with the assumption that one author will not often be flagrantly inconsistent with himself, then there is all the more reason to assume that if the Bible is the product of the Holy Spirit there can be no inconsistency. Thus a person is always on firm ground if he explains one passage by another even if it means explaining away what may be the most simple or natural meaning of a text. As a matter of fact, even to suppose that the most simple or natural meaning of a text is contradictory to some other quite clear passage is blasphemy.

Calvin's exegetical work is filled with passages in which he brings one verse to bear on the interpretation of another. One statement by Isaiah, for example, has had various interpretations. It happens that Paul quotes this statement in I Corinthians. By

---

* Com. John, Argument (C.O. 47.viii). Cf. Com. Matt. 28:16 (C.O. 45.820): "As we have already had frequent opportunities of perceiving—it was not the intention of the Evangelists to embrace every part of the history; because the Holy Spirit, who guided their pen, has thought fit to compose such a summary as we see out of their united testimonies." In the same vein are the comments on Matt. 2:1 (C.O. 45.81): "The Spirit of God, who had appointed the Evangelists to be his clerks, appears purposely to have regulated their style in such a manner, that they all wrote one and the same history, with the most perfect agreement, but in different ways. It was intended, that the truth of God should more clearly and strikingly appear, when it was manifest that his witnesses did not speak by a preconcerted plan, but that each of them separately, without paying any attention to another, wrote freely and honestly what the Holy Spirit dictated."

all means, the debate should be ended with this discovery. "For where shall we find a surer or more faithful interpreter than the Spirit of God of this authoritative declaration, which He himself dictated to Isaiah—in the exposition which He has furnished by the mouth of Paul?"[48] In another place we are led into a more complete understanding of the Psalmist—an understanding we would never have seen if we had been left with nothing more than the words of the Psalmist—by Paul's quotation in Romans.

> But David goes farther, declaring that the whole life of man is subjected to God's wrath and curse, except in so far as he vouchsafes of his own free grace to receive them into his favour; of which the Spirit who spake by David is an assured interpreter and witness to us by the mouth of Paul, (Rom. 4:6.) Had Paul not used this testimony, never would his readers have penetrated the real meaning of the prophet.[49]

The most interesting passage of harmonization on the basis of this principle is found at that point where Calvin acknowledges the current debate over Paul and James. It is an incredible situation as far as Calvin is concerned: "What then? Will they draw Paul into a controversy with James? If they consider James as a minister of Christ, his declarations must be understood in some sense not at variance with Christ when speaking by the mouth of Paul."[50] Paul, of course, argued that Abraham was justified by faith and not by works, whereas James said that he was justified by works and not by faith only. Calvin observes,

> That the Spirit is not inconsistent with himself is a certain truth. . . . I deny, therefore, that the assertion of James, which they hold up against us as an impenetrable shield, affords them the least support. . . . It is not his design, then, to diminish, in any respect the virtue of true faith, but to show the folly of these triblers, who were content with arrogating to themselves the vain image of it, and securely abandoned themselves to every vice.[51]

He then brings the debate to a close in the next paragraph: "If we wish to make James consistent with the rest of the Scriptures, and even with himself, we must understand the word 'justify' in a different signification from that in which it is used by Paul."[52]

Continuing the exposition, Calvin declares that Paul has followed the proper chronology in placing Abraham's justification long before his works. On the other hand, since it would be "unlawful" to suppose that James "improperly inverted the order of events," we must conclude that James did not mean by justification "that the patriarch deserved to be accounted righteous." He concludes that James was speaking of a declaration of righteousness before men, not God. What he intended to say was that one who is justified proves his justification in good works. "In a word, he is not disputing concerning the method of justification, but requiring of believers a righteousness manifested in good works."[53]

It may be said, then, that the work of the Holy Spirit in the writers of the Bible was to produce a scripture free from all human admixtures in all its parts. This was accomplished through some form of "dictation," with the result that any part of it—or any word, for that matter—could be taken as having the full weight of divine authority. As an additional substantiation, we have noted that this conviction in the authorship of the Spirit was the basis for Calvin's belief in the unity of the Bible and the authority for the exegete to make full use of his ingenuity in harmonizing the various portions of scripture. It may safely be said that this is the extent of Calvin's explicit statements about the work of the Spirit in the writers of the Bible.

Beyond Literalism

It cannot be said, however, that we have exhausted all the material in Calvin that might be applicable to his view on the inspiration of the scriptures. As a matter of fact, there are any number of places where Calvin, in speaking of the scriptures, does not feel called upon to use the language which we have seen was so characteristic. These are the passages in which his interest is more general or broadly thematic and in which he refers to "Christ," "the gospel," or "the promises" rather than to the "words" or "dictation" of the Spirit. By interpreting Calvin on the basis of these passages, J. K. S. Reid while commenting on an important passage on the setting down of the patriarchial tradition writes:

The statement is made in terms of knowledge; but it is clear that Calvin has in mind no merely intellectual knowledge and no purely epistemological relation between the prophets and their Creator and Redeemer. The "internal knowledge" that is later added to the knowledge of their Creator, he says specifically, "vivifies dead souls." It is revelation that is here the subject of inquiry; and revelation in the sense not of "information" about God, but of the impartation of God Himself to named individuals.[54]

Whether or not the disclaimer of a "purely epistemological relation between the prophets and their Creater and Redeemer" is an adequate appraisal of Calvin's position will be discussed in the chapter on the content and character of knowledge. At this juncture, it is necessary to see the validity of Reid's emphasis on revelation over against information on the giving of God Himself as distinguished from merely a deposit of something about God.

Wilhelm Niesel is most interested in making this point in his book *The Theology of Calvin*.[55] He compares Calvin's introduction to the *Institutes* with his introduction to the Genevan translation of the Bible. The introduction to the *Institutes,* as we have seen, indicates the author's claim to give a summary of the teaching of the Bible as an introduction to the study of the Bible itself. The introduction to the Genevan translation proclaims the importance of Bible study and—what is more important here—describes Calvin's conception of the end of Bible study. That end is to learn "to place our trust in God and to walk in the fear of Him, and—since Jesus Christ is the end of the law and the prophets and the essence of the gospel—of aspiring to no other aim but to know Him, since we realize that we cannot deviate from that path in the slightest degree without going astray."[56] Niesel calls attention to a number of other similar statements by Calvin. When we read the Bible it must be with the intention of finding Christ in it. Perhaps the most telling declaration by Calvin is found in one of his sermons: "When we read Scripture our aim must be to be truly edified in faith and in the fear of the Lord, to become drawn to our Lord Jesus Christ and to recognize that God has imparted Himself to us in Him that we may possess Him as our in-

heritance."[58] When Calvin comments on John 5:39, he directs
the reader to hold fast to that which speaks of and leads him to
Christ.[59] It is well known that Calvin, as had been the case with
theologians for centuries, read Christ freely and profusely into
the Old Testament, but it is important to reiterate that Calvin un-
derstod the law, indeed the whole of the Christian religion, to be
dead without Christ.[60] Elsewhere we are told that the office of the
Spirit is to exhibit Christ and that the doctrine about which he is
speaking is the doctrine of the Gospel.[61]

All of this, it is clear, is relating the scriptures to the focal
point of the *Institutes,* the doctrine of faith. As we have seen,*
the exposition of faith, although it is not a doctrine from which
all others are systematically derived, may be looked upon as the
vital nerve of his theology, and that doctrine to which he relates
most others. That is the case, we now see, with his understanding
of the Bible, and it bears on our understanding of the inspiration
of scripture. The connection, however, is one of silence. Calvin,
when he speaks of the scriptures broadly in terms of "Christ,"
does not find it necessary to support this with the language of
dictation. We cannot say that he thereby distinguished the two
in his own mind. Incontrovertibly, he would never have separated
the two approaches. Nonetheless, there is a difference between
them.

In Part III we will see that Calvin used the scriptures in different ways, corresponding to the different ways just noted in
which he spoke about the Bible as a whole. As for the present
discussion, it is impossible to evaluate the data and stand solidly
on one side or the other of the debate about Calvin's view of the
inspiration of the Bible. On the one hand, we simply cannot read
off as figurative language everything he says about the work of the
Spirit in the writers of the record. On the other hand, neither can
we overlook as insignificant or unrelated all that he has to say
about Christ as the key to the scriptures or the relation of the Bible
as a whole to the promises or the doctrine of faith. If we are to be
true to the sources, we can only say that he clearly sets forth both

* Above, pp. 40–41.

positions, now emphasizing one and now the other. The question of the theory of inspiration in Calvin can perhaps be most adequately resolved in terms of the double emphasis. Those who do not interpret Calvin as a literalist make much of his emphasis on Christ, the promises, and faith. Their point cannot be denied. Insofar as the knowledge of faith is concerned, Calvin does not need and does not use a theory of verbal inspiration. Neither can we deny or explain away the strong emphasis on the totality of scripture and particularly on all its individual parts. So we must also say: insofar as the wider knowledge is concerned, Calvin both needs and is forced to use scripture in such a way as to emphasize its literal inerrancy.

The Work of the Spirit
in the Believer

Unlike the topic discussed in the previous chapter, the subject to which we turn our attention now is clearly and explicitly developed by Calvin. If Calvin's conception of the work of the Spirit in the writers of the Bible calls for some little speculation on the part of his interpreters because the material is scattered and incomplete, that should not be the case at all in regard to his conception of the work of the Spirit in the believer. As a matter of fact, our author devotes two full chapters in the *Institutes* to this theme. The seventh chapter of Book I is entitled: "The Testimony of the Spirit Necessary to Confirm the Scripture, in Order to the Complete Establishment of Its Authority. The Suspension of Its Authority on the Judgment of the Church, an Impious Fiction." In addition to this the first chapter of Book III is given over to a discussion of "What Is Declared Concerning Christ Rendered Profitable to Us by the Secret Operation of the Spirit."

On the face of it, then, the present discussion presents not nearly so formidable a problem as the preceding one. Perhaps it would be more accurate to say only that the material for this topic dictates a different methodology than that employed in the former chapter. Here we must obviously begin with an exposition of these two key chapters in the *Institutes*.

When Calvin commented on the new covenant as it is described in Hebrews 8:10 he wrote: "There are two main parts in this covenant; the first regards the gratuitous remission of sins; and the other, the inward renovation of the heart; there is a third which depends on the second, and that is the illumination of the mind as to the knowledge of God."[1] In these three parts is comprehended the subject matter of the two chapters in the *Institutes* on the work of the Spirit in the believer. The chapter in Book III deals primarily with the work of the Spirit in persuading one of God's gratuitous remission of one's sins, and it touches upon the work of the Spirit in regeneration inasmuch as regeneration always follows hard upon faith. Neither faith nor regeneration, of course, can be understood as human possibilities or achievements. They are words of the Spirit. The chapter in Book I, on the other hand, deals, as its title suggests, with the work of the Spirit in confirming and establishing the authority of the scripture. Since the Bible is the source of our more complete and our only reliable knowledge of God, this particular work of the Spirit corresponds to the third part of the covenant.

The Work of the Spirit in Faith and Regeneration
(*Institutes*, Book III, Chapter i)

Before embarking on a summary of the material in the introductory chapter to the third book of the *Institutes* it is important to recall that the main divisions of this work are patterned after the main divisions of the Apostles' Creed. Thus Book II is, broadly speaking, a discussion of Christ, the heart of which is an exaltation of Christ as the one through whom the grace of God for salvation has been merited for us. The first words in Book III pick up this theme and ask how it is that men can enjoy these blessings which have been won through the Son of God. One thing is necessary: we must be united with Christ. "As long as there is a separation between Christ and us, all that he suffered and performed for the salvation of mankind is useless and unavailing to us. To communicate to us what he received from his Father, he must, therefore, become ours, and dwell within us." It is taken for granted that this union and the consequent enjoyment of salvation are achieved by faith. Not everyone, however, has faith. Therefore, "reason itself teaches us to proceed further, and to inquire into the secret energy of the Spirit, by which we are introduced to the enjoyment of Christ and all his benefits."[2] We are to understand, then, that the discussion of salvation is by no means finished with the discussion of Christ in Book II. It is only finished when we recognize that the work of the Spirit is complementary to the work of Christ.* Christ came thus by water and blood, that the Spirit may testify concerning him, in order that the salvation procured by him may not be lost to us."[3] Then follow the ever ready references to various passages of scripture, after which he concludes the paragraph clearly and forcefully: "The Holy Spirit is the bond by which Christ efficaciously unites us to himself."[4]

As observed, the reason Calvin gives for looking to the Spirit as the means by which Christ's benefits are made available to us is that not everyone has faith. Faith, in Calvin's understanding, is not a human possibility. Why one man comes to faith and another does not can only be explained by comprehending faith as a gift of God. If in Book II he explained how Christ merited salvation for us who cannot merit it for ourselves through works of the law, then in Book III he intends to show how, because we cannot on the basis of our own strength come to enjoy this salvation through faith, God creates this faith in us through the secret operation of his Spirit in our hearts.

There is, however, another reason for attributing faith to the work of the Spirit. Calvin puts it this way: "Till our minds are fixed on the Spirit, Christ remains of no value to us; because we look at him as an object of cold speculation without us, and therefore at a great distance from us."[5] Salvation is not something purely objective. This is not to say that Calvin did not conceive the work of salvation to have taken place objectively in the sphere of God—that is, outside of human subjective feeling and apprehension. Of course, Calvin conceived it to be objective in that sense. That is the main thrust of Book II, the discussion of Christ, and Book III, the discussion of the Spirit. Christ and the Spirit

---

* E. A. Dowey's book, *The Knowledge of God in Calvin's Theology*, defends the thesis that Calvin's *Institutes* can best be understood in terms of the twofold knowledge of God, the *duplex cognitio Dei*—namely, the knowledge of God the Creator and the knowledge of God the Redeemer—rather than in terms of Calvin's own division into four books. That this is the case should be clear by the fact that Calvin himself acknowledges no break between Book II and Book III. On the contrary, as noted here, there is only an easy transition within the same general topic, salvation.

are not inside men; they are divine beings. The point, however, is that a man cannot by himself appropriate the benefits of Christ because he will inevitably look on Christ as something outside himself and nothing more. Christ, however, must become one with us. He must dwell in our hearts. This is the work of the Spirit; it cannot, to Calvin's mind, be conceived in any other way. It must be admitted that if one is to speak of the Spirit at all, this is, indeed, an appropriate way in which to speak. The operation of the Spirit is always internal by the very nature of the case. In this instance, nothing could be more fit than to attribute to the Spirit that work which enables one to confess with deep internal conviction, "*My God*," or to be convinced that what Christ has done was done "for *me*."

In this connection, let us observe that Calvin considered this to be the principal work of the Spirit. "But faith, being his principal work, is the object principally referred to in the most frequent expressions of his power and operation; because it is the only medium by which he leads us into the light of the gospel."[6] We will want to bear this in mind at a later point, but it is sufficient here to recognize that faith, being a supernatural gift, is brought into being in the hearts of men by the secret operation of the Holy Spirit; and this is the major work of that Spirit.

The chapter which we are now considering includes also a few scattered statements about the work of the Spirit in regeneration. Calvin is intensely interested in the Christian life, and he exercised extreme care in seeking to acquit the new movement of the charge of antinomianism.* So in this chapter he emphasizes that when the Spirit works in the heart to produce faith, it also works for the consequent renewal of life. That is why the Spirit is called "the Spirit of holiness" (Rom. 1:4) because "he is the seed and root of a heavenly life within us."[7] This work is also derived from various other names of the Spirit. It is because of righteousness that he is said to be "life" (Rom. 8:10).[8] Furthermore, "since by his secret showers he makes us fertile in producing the fruits of righteousness, he is frequently called 'water.' "[9] The Spirit is

---

* It was for this reason that Calvin inserted his discussion of the Christian life between his chapter on faith and his discussion of justification.

"fire" (Luke 3:16) because he burns away our vices and enflames our hearts with a zeal for righteousness,[10] and he is a "fountain" (John 4:14) "because by the breath of his power he inspires us with Divine life, so that we are not now actuated from ourselves, but directed by his agency and influence; so that if there be any good in us, it is the fruit of his grace, whereas our characters without him are darkness of mind and perverseness of heart."[11]

The Work of the Spirit in Confirming the Scriptures (*Institutes*, Book I, Chapter vii)

Book I of the *Institutes* deals with the creature's knowledge of God the Creator. After an introductory chapter relating the knowledge of God and the knowledge of oneself, there are four chapters discussing the knowledge of God available in the creation, including the individual conscience. In a sense this is a hypothetical discussion inasmuch as sin so universally reigns in the human heart that men inevitably obscure or pervert that knowledge which in itself is so clear. The main purpose of these chapters, of course, is to echo Paul in denying excuse to all who are ignorant of God. Chapter VI then shows that—the case being what it is—it is necessary for us to have the guidance of scripture in order to come to a reliable knowledge of God the Creator.

At this point, however, a formidable problem presents itself. How is one to know that the Bible is the only reliable source of knowledge about God? Calvin must be careful in answering this question. The Church of Rome also exalts the scriptures, but it claims that one can be assured of its authority only through the judgment of the Church. For Calvin, however, this is an impossible position because it subordinates the divine authority to a human judgment about it. For the same reason Calvin is hesitant to rest the case for the divinity of scripture on rational disputation. This hesitancy, let us note, does not in any way minimize the weight of the evidence pointing to the divine original of scripture. On the contrary, although Calvin disclaims any talent as a debater, he is convinced that the evidence in this case is so strong that he could easily overthrow the most witty and skillful.[12] Nonetheless, the authority of scripture, being divine, must not rest upon the reasons of men.

Calvin devotes more than half of this short chapter to an attack upon these two possible ways of establishing belief in the Bible. The case against the first rests on temporal priority: The Church is "built upon the foundation of the apostles and prophets" (Eph. 2:20) rather than vice versa.[13] If it were the other way around, then would our faith be ridiculous, having "only a precarious authority depending on the favour of men!"[14] To lend even more weight to his argument Calvin explains carefully the statement by Augustine that he would not believe the authority of the Bible except under the influence of the authority of the Church. This, asserts Calvin, does not mean that faith in the scriptures is dependent on the authority of the Church but only that the consent of the Church is a valuable assistance in assuring the individual in his belief.[15]

The point of the whole polemic—against human reason as well as against the Church—is that if one is to avoid "perpetual doubt," the conviction of the divinity of scripture must be found in a source higher than anything human, "the secret testimony of the Holy Spirit."[16] In a way, rational arguments are more conclusive than declarations of the Church because they are conclusive in themselves, but no matter how conclusive they may be, they cannot "fix in their hearts that assurance which is essential to true piety."[17] Human reasons are fallible; moreover, the mind which is convinced by them is fickle. Only one thing is certain to remove doubt. If God has spoken in the Bible, then God himself must convince us of this fact. "God alone is a sufficient witness of himself in his word."[18]

Therefore Calvin must speak of the scripture as being "self-authenticated."[19] It carries with it its own evidence. The only way we can know "the divine original of the Scripture" is by a divine act within us.[20] The description of this event taxes the human language. Calvin finds that his "language falls far short of a just explication of the subject," but he takes heart in the fact that what he says so poorly is "what every believer experiences in his heart."[21] Because this knowledge comes only through the testimony of the Holy Spirit, one should not be disturbed if many people do not believe it. It comes only to those to whom it has been given.[22]

If, as we have seen, the Spirit is quite appropriate as a symbol referring to that which effects faith, it is not so obviously pertinent to the production of a belief in the divine original of scripture. The work of the Spirit in relation to faith can be expressed in three closely related statements. First, it effects salvation for an individual. What God has done in Christ is directed toward the individual through the work of the Spirit. Second, coincident with this work the Spirit also effects a subjective apprehension of it in the individual. One is persuaded that what has happened in Christ has happened "for me," *erga me*. Also, through this work of the Spirit one is united to Christ by such an intimate and secure bond that the union can never be severed.

The work of the Spirit in relation to the confirmation of scripture can also be expressed in three statements of a similar nature. For one thing, in this work the Spirit effects knowledge in the believer. Calvin, of course, speaks of faith as knowledge; but the knowledge involved in this work of the Spirit is much broader as it is also more detailed. It is, in short, everything that is set forth in the Bible. Second, in this work the Spirit convinces one that he (the Spirit) is the real author of the Bible. Finally, though the language referring to the work of the Spirit is internal, the product of the work is rather objective. Once this work has been accomplished, one can, without being plagued by doubt, take the whole Bible as irrefutable knowledge. In the work of faith the Spirit produces a solid persuasion within one which has to do with one's own self. In confirming the scripture it produces a certainty about something quite removed from oneself.

These two works of the Spirit in the believer are thus of different characters, and they are analogous to the two poles between which Calvin oscillates in speaking of the Bible and its inspiration. When Calvin speaks of the scriptures in terms of Christ, the promises, the gospel, or God's gratuitous mercy, it is not necessary for him to use, nor does he in fact use, a doctrine of verbal inspiration. The work of the Spirit in such instances may be considered identical to the work of the Spirit described in Book III, Chapter i.

There is this difference only: In the case of the writers of the Bible there was a more complete immediacy in the totality of the work. Not only was the work of the Spirit immediate in persuading their hearts of the veracity of the promises toward them, but also the perception of the promises themselves was immediate, coming directly from God or Christ. In the case of other believers, the perception of the promises comes indirectly through the witness of those who received them directly—the Bible. In this sense, the Bible is, indeed, a real witness to the revelation.

On the other hand, when Calvin uses the language of the dictation theory of inspiration, there is a certain relation to his conception of the work of the Spirit in the believer described in Book I, Chapter vii. In this case it is not an identical work; rather it is complementary. First, the Spirit guides the pens of the writers of the Bible; then he moves men to recognize the fact that he has done so. Even though the work is not identical, however, it is interesting to note that the character is similar. In both instances the work is rather mechanical and objective. The apprehension by the subject under the influence of the Spirit has no material effect upon the object. In the one case, all that is involved is the transmission of what is apprehended. In the other, there is only an acknowledgment of what has been transmitted. On the contrary, in the work of the Spirit in faith, the apprehension by the subject involves not just an awareness that the state of affairs is thus and so, but more particularly that God's gratuitous mercy is directed *toward me*.

Of course, Calvin mixed somewhat the two works of the Spirit in the believer. In each of the two chapters in the *Institutes* he includes a statement which properly relates to the other. In the discussion of the confirmation of scripture he writes, "I pass over many things at present, because this subject will present itself for discussion again in another place. Only let it be known here, that that alone is true faith which the Spirit of God seals in our hearts."[23] In the first chapter of Book III he introduces near the end a statement about the Spirit as productive of truth and wisdom:

> He ascribes to him [the Holy Spirit] the peculiar office of suggesting to their minds all the oral instructions which he had

given them. For in vain would the light present itself to the blind, unless this Spirit of understanding would open their mental eyes; so that he may be justly called the key with which the treasures of the kingdom of heaven are unlocked to us; and his illumination constitutes our mental eyes to behold them.[24]

Nonetheless, it must be remembered that Calvin considered the work of the Spirit in confirming faith to be his principal work.

One other observation may be made. If we pay attention to Calvin's division of the *Institutes* we will have to say that the discussion of the work of the Spirit in Book I is displaced. Book III is that division in which he proposes to discuss the work of the Spirit. There he begins with the discussion of the work of the Spirit in effecting faith and follows that with a discussion of faith proper and the various doctrines which follow directly from faith: regeneration, justification, prayer, election, and resurrection. It must be said, I think, that even if Calvin could have deferred the discussion of the work of the Spirit in confirming the scriptures to what apparently should be its proper place—Book III—it would be out of place. It must come where it does because Calvin's concept of theology is heteronomous and authoritative. Thus at the very beginning he must set up this authority which is certain because it is circumscribed on every side by divine activity. The first five chapters of the *Institutes* are not materially related to the whole. They simply clear the way. The real beginning is the sixth chapter, discussing the necessity of the scripture, which is followed by the exposition of the work of the Spirit in confirming the scriptures. This is the springboard of the whole work. On the other hand, the first two chapters of Book III are the vital nerve of the theology. In effect, then, there are two principles governing the *Institutes*, not entirely distinct, not entirely dissimilar, yet possessing different characters and operating on the basis of different presuppositions.

The Spirit and the Illumination of the Mind and Heart:
The Holy Spirit as Teacher

In our examination of the two chapters which Calvin devotes to a discussion of the work of the Spirit in the believer, we have not exhausted all that our author has to say on the subject. As a matter of fact, there are two further works of the Spirit in the believer, both of which are related to the confirmation of scripture. They themselves are closely related: the work of the Spirit as teacher and the work of the Spirit in interpretation.

In reading Calvin one may soon come to think that his favorite descriptive word for the Spirit is "Teacher." Somehow men are always being taught, and if it is sometimes God who teaches or even Christ, then that is only because Calvin was quite free—most of the time—in substituting the first or the second person of the Trinity when he would normally have been expected to refer to the third person. In a comment on Psalm 119:125 Calvin explains how it is that we are taught by God. First, God does it "by illuminating with sound knowledge (*sana intelligentia*), and then he renders us "docile by the secret influence of his Spirit."[25]

This illumination and this docility often appear to be identical with the confirmation of scripture. In these instances the work of the Holy Spirit is that of convincing and persuading. This is the case in the comment on Isaiah 54:13 where Calvin joins external preaching and "the internal efficacy of the Holy Spirit" as the way in which the Lord teaches us.[26] The only difference here is that preaching has been substituted for the word, but it is not a serious difference since preaching anything other than the word was inconceivable to Calvin.

If Calvin occasionally makes a statement which implies that the teaching of the Holy Spirit is apart from the word, then he is quick to correct himself. At one point in the commentary on the Psalms he speaks of the gift of inward illumination. The comment is on "Blessed is the man whom thou hast instructed" (Ps. 94:12), and one is almost led to think instruction is apart from the scriptures. It might be, but Calvin carefully adds at the end: "Afterwards the Psalmist adds, that this wisdom, which is imparted by God inwardly, is, at the same time, set forth and made known in the Scriptures."[27] In his polemic against the spiritualists in the *Institutes*, he makes clear his conviction that since the Spirit cannot be inconsistent with himself, he at no time gives us inward instructions contrary to what is in his word, and, furthermore, that since what is in his word is sufficient, he never gives us instructions which can be added to his word. The Spirit is a teacher, but he only teaches us what is already in his word. "Nothing more is to be expected from his Spirit, than that he will enlighten our minds (*mentes nostras illuminet*) to discover the truth of his doctrine."[28] "And if we ought to follow the guidance of the Spirit, where he leaves us, there we ought to stop and as it were to fix our standing."[29]

Although the Spirit will add nothing to his word he does face a larger task than simply causing men to acknowledge him in it. Because "we are all blind by nature"[30] he must give us a "sound mind (*sanam mentem*)"[31] to understand what is in the word.

> Since, then, he affirms that he would give them a heart to understand (*se daturum illis cor ut intelligat*), we hence learn (*colligimus*) that men are by nature blind, and also that when they are blinded by the devil, they cannot return to the right way, and that they cannot be otherwise capable of light than by having God to illuminate them by his Spirit (*Deus illuminat spiritu suo*).[32]

In this we are essentially like the apostles who heard everything Christ said but did not understand until their hearts were enlightened and their darkness was driven away.[33] Christ was a teacher to them, but he also "employed the secret revelation of the Spirit." In short, "he taught the apostles efficaciously."[34] God employs the Spirit in this way when he begins to restore his Church. The Roman Church, it will be remembered, had not forsaken the Bible before the beginning of the Reformation. Indeed, Luther inherited his biblicism from the Nominalists. There are times, then, when the acknowledgment of scripture is not enough. When the Church understands scripture improperly, God himself undertakes the office of teacher and by connecting the external voice with the secret operation of his Spirit effects renewal.[35]

Men, of themselves, are blinder than moles with respect to the things of God, and they are constantly in danger of making mistakes, drawing a wrong meaning, or going astray. The Spirit must do more than confirm the scripture; it must "illuminate the understanding (*illustrare mentes*)"[36] in order that we may know the meaning of that which we know to be the word of God.

The Spirit of Discernment: The Holy Spirit as Interpreter

This introduces us by indirection to the most formidable problem involved in Calvin's doctrine of the authority of scripture. To say that the Bible is a divine product and that it is acknowledged as such through a divine activity in men lends to the principle of authority a certainty apparently protected on every side. However, the scriptures are not always clear. To be edifying they must be interpreted.

Although Calvin thought the Bible was a good deal more clear than most of his opponents did, he realized that it is not so clear that it needs no explanation. On the contrary, it was to this task that he devoted his life. The introduction of the necessity of interpretation, however, did not at all pierce his bulwark of certainty. Interpretation is also the work of the Spirit. Where the explanation of the scripture is correct, the Spirit of Discernment has been at work.

This is entirely consistent with Calvin's other reasoning about the Spirit. If only the Spirit can confirm the fact that it is author of the word, then we may also say that "the Spirit of God, from whom the doctrine of the gospel comes, is its only true interpreter, to open it up for us."[37] "The Spirit, who spoke by the prophets, is the only true interpreter of himself."[38] In this manner Calvin joins word and Spirit in a way different from but analogous to the way previously noted:

> For the Scripture is the true touchstone whereby all doctrines must be tried. If any man say that this kind of trial is doubtful, forasmuch as the Scripture is oftentimes doubtful, and is interpreted divers ways, I say, that we must also add the judgment of the Spirit, who is, not without cause, called the Spirit of discretion (discernment, *discretionis*). But the faithful must judge of every doctrine no otherwise than out of and according to, the Scriptures, having the Spirit for their leader and guide.[39]

The believer with the word in his hand realizes that it contains a wisdom which is beyond his ability to comprehend. He does not, because of this, lay it aside. On the contrary, he reads it diligently, depends upon the enlightenment of the Spirit, and earnestly hopes for an interpreter.[40]

With this we are brought to the other side of the problem of interpretation. Interpretation is not left entirely, or even primarily, to the individual. There are special men, pastors and teachers, who are given the task of interpreting for others. "We must remember, that the Scripture is not only given us, but that interpreters and teachers are also added, to be helps to us."[41] Ideally, God should govern his people and interpret his mind to them, but since he is not with us by a "visible presence," "he uses the ministry of men whom he employs as his delegates, not to transfer his right and honour to them, but only that he may himself do his work by their lips."[42]

The Church and her leaders assume a position of considerable authority in Calvin's theology. "We are certain," he writes, "as long as we continue in the bosom of the Church, that we shall remain in possession of the truth."[43] Anyone who withdraws himself from the Church is nothing other than "a traitor and apostate from religion."[44] When the Church declares a sentence, "God has testified that it is no other than a declaration of his sentence, and that what they do on earth shall be ratified in Heaven."[45] Preachers who interpret the word of God are to be listened to as if God himself were speaking.[46]

In all this, however, it is necessary to remember that Calvin defines the Church as that place where the word is rightly preached and the sacraments properly administered.[47] Moreover, if the Church is valued highly, it is also because it is there that the Spirit of God reigns. If pastors are given authority comparable in its description to that given to the word itself, it is because God has connected preaching with his Spirit.[48] For this reason "the majesty of God is, as it were, indissolubly connected with the public preaching of his truth."[49]

If one desires to be a preacher or teacher, one must have this Spirit. "Whoever then desires to be deemed a servant of God, and a teacher in his Church, must have this seal . . . ; he must be endued with the Spirit of God."[50] If interpretation is necessary and men are set apart to do this work for the Church, then it must not be separated from the Spirit.[51] If it should be, the pillars connecting the structure to its foundation would be removed and the whole would collapse. There could be no certainty at all if the Spirit were not working through those who interpret.

This same thing, of course, can be said of councils. Calvin believed that on many matters the most certain way to come to a true decision is by a lawfully constituted council of the Church. But, again, a council is only authoritative when the Holy Spirit reigns over its sessions. Calvin accepted the dicta of the first four ecumenical councils because he thought they included nothing that is not in the word and because he was convinced that the Holy Spirit was working in the deliberations. On the other hand, he had rather harsh words in reply to the claim that the deliberations at the Council of Trent were governed by the Holy Spirit.[52] Calvin believed in councils, but it was necessary that they be governed by the Spirit in the interpretation of the word. Only thus could full certainty remain for the believer.

After the work of the Spirit through the lawfully constituted interpreters and councils of the Church, there is a corresponding work of the Spirit in regular believers. Calvin was not an individualist in the sense that he thought the individual had the right to judge every interpretation or every decision of a council. Yet to a certain extent this is the case. In his comment on I John 2:27 he indicates that a further office of the Spirit is that "he endues us with judgment and discernment (*iudicis et discretione*), lest we should be deceived by lies."[53] Earlier in the same comment he describes the Spirit as "the only fit corrector and approver of doctrine (*solus est idoneus doctrinae censor et approbatur*), who seals it on our hearts, so that we may certainly know that God speaks (*ut certo sciamus Deum loqui*)."[54]

If it be the case that the Holy Spirit works through pastors and teachers to interpret the word rightly and through us to discern, correct, and approve that which we are taught, then only one question remains: How do we know when we or others have this Spirit of Discernment?

Discerning the Spirit of Discernment

 The adequacy of Calvin's principle of authority and the solidity of the certainty derived from it depend in large measure upon a successful handling of this question. It is not given a systematic treatment in the *Institutes*, but it is dealt with repeatedly and often rather extensively in the commentaries. From these separate passages we must search for Calvin's answer to the problem. Because his comments are suggested by particular passages of scripture, the total impact of all his statements is something of a maze. Many tests are suggested—whether or not one has a call from God, says what is edifying, manifests the Spirit in one's conduct, speaks in the name of God, glorifies God and debases oneself, etc. The most curious thing, however, is that when all his statements are weighed together, there is no one public test to which one can turn without reservation.

The difficulty of pinning down Calvin's answer to this problem may be readily seen by taking a close look at one of his extended comments on the issue. Of Matthew 7:16, "By their fruits you shall know them," Calvin writes, "Had not this mark of distinction been added, we might have called in question the authority of all teachers without exception." Thus the beginning of the exposition holds good promise for some concrete suggestion. As Calvin develops his ideas, we find that he first explains the meaning of "fruits." It would be inadequate to think of this in relation to the life of a teacher. There are too many who pretend sanctity. To be sure, hypocrisy is sooner or later detected, but nonetheless Christ did not intend that we should use a criterion so susceptible to misunderstanding. "Fruits," therefore, must be understood as referring to the manner of teaching. In essence this is to test one by asking, "Who is glorified?" It also includes doctrine. If some complain that they are not capable of judging doctrine, Calvin answers, "Believers are never deprived of the Spirit of wisdom, where his assistance is needful . . . provided they give themselves up wholly to his direction." Even with this one must remember that doctrines must be measured against the Bible as the standard. In all of this, titles and church positions go for nought.

The exposition concludes with the statement that only willful blindness can prevent proper judgment.[55]

Calvin mentions one's manner of life as a possible test, but then quickly qualifies it. In another place, the qualification does not appear. That is where he comments on Psalm 18:21, "For I have kept the ways of Jehovah." Calvin admits that the hypocrites speak in the same vein, but he claims that everyone could plainly see that it was true with David.[56] It was most natural, however, for our author to qualify this test by another one. In another place, for example, he begins in much the same way, declaring, "Faithful ministers differ much from them [false ones], who declare nothing of themselves but what they really manifest in their conduct." Not long after that, however, he must add, "It cannot be but that every one who really fears and obeys God, knows him in his word."[57]

In the extended passage in Matthew, Calvin apparently left standing without qualification the test on the basis of who is glorified. One gathers that Calvin put a good deal of confidence in this criterion. At one point in his letter to Francis I he let his case for the Reformed teaching rest on it. "Paul's direction, that every prophecy be framed 'according to the analogy of faith,'" he writes, "has fixed an invariable standard by which all interpretation of Scripture ought to be tried." Then he claims the victory. "For what is more consistent with faith than to acknowledge ourselves naked of all virtue, that we may be clothed by God; empty of all good, that we may be filled by him," etc.[58] In contrast with this Calvin asserts that in the whole Roman Catholic system there is nothing but self-seeking. The Council of Trent opened with a declaration of humility and repentance among the delegates, but Calvin shows nothing but disdain for this, considering it only an outward show.[59] Here it seems we have a criterion which is thoroughly objective. "Now, if the whole doctrine of the Pope be examined, even the blind will see that he has come in his own name."[60]

In this passage the question, "Who is glorified?" is equated with the question, "In whose name does he come?" This is equally a necessity for the valid teacher. "Whoever assumes a right to instruct us, must speak in the name of God or of Christ."[61] Yet if this is to be equated with the previous test, then they both must be qualified, because false prophets, including papists, Mohammed, and even the Egyptians claim to speak in the name of God.[62] As a matter of fact, Calvin finds that we are specifically enjoined to put such claims to the test. They must be proved. The proof is in the word of God. "We have the word of the Lord, which ought especially to be consulted. When, therefore, false spirits pretend the name of God, we must inquire from the Scriptures whether things are so."[63]

Closely related is the question whether one has been called by God. "What is asserted about John is required in all the teachers of the Church, that they be called by God; so that the authority of teaching may not be founded on any other than on God alone."[64] Again, however, there is no foolproof procedure for ascertaining such a call. For one thing, the teacher must "not bring anything of his own, but faithfully deliver, as from hand to hand, what he has received from God."[65] Calvin notes that there might be some perplexity on the matter even then, so he adds: "We now then perceive what Jeremiah had in view: he had before said, that none were to be attended to, except they who were sent and spoke from the mouth of God, but he now explains what he meant, even that the Law contained the whole sum of wisdom."[66]

In one place (comments on John 3:2) Calvin discusses miracles as a proof of the authority of the teacher. However, he quickly qualifies this, because impostors and the Antichrist himself seek to bewitch men by wonderful signs. Nonetheless, Calvin is not willing to discount entirely the place of miracles in corroborating teaching. He gives them a place, but in such a way that one can hardly assess it as an objective test. "When the eyes are opened [!] and the light of spiritual wisdom shines, miracles are a sufficiently powerful attestation of the presence of God."[67]

In another place the test is whether the teacher has been anointed.[68] A teacher is anointed "if he is endued with the gifts which are necessary for that office." What, then, are these "gifts"? They are "the graces of the Spirit and the ability which the calling demands." If he has these, "he actually has the Spirit." Then he ought to be heard "as a public minister who has come from heaven."

Most often in discussing the tests of the Spirit in those who interpret, Calvin comes back to the word. This has been seen in some of the passages discussed above. He is more direct about it elsewhere. "Those only are deemed by God to be the faithful pastors of the Church, who . . . rightly judge and according to the law of God. . . . The law then is alone that by which we can distinguish the precious from the worthless."[69] This, then, is the only criterion, but it is also the problem. We began with an acknowledgment of the necessity of interpretation and saw how Calvin maintains the full strength of his principle of authority by attributing interpretation itself to the Spirit. Now we find that the only reliable way in which to know that Spirit is on the basis of that which the Spirit is to interpret.

At times even the Bible is not considered a sufficient test by Calvin. In I John 4:1 the reader is urged to "try the Spirits." People are bound to ask, Calvin points out, where this discernment comes from. "They who answer, that the word of God is the rule by which everything that men bring forward ought to be tried, say something, but not the whole. I grant that doctrines ought to be tested by God's word; but except the Spirit of wisdom be present, to have God's word in our hands will avail little or nothing, for its meaning will not appear to us."[70] Calvin then goes on to speak of the necessity of the Spirit of Discretion, and claims that one will never be left destitute of him if one ask God for him. Realizing, however, that this Spirit is not exactly concrete and clear, he moves again back toward the word. "But the Spirit will only thus guide us to a right discrimination, when we render all our thoughts subject to God's word (*si omnes nostros sensus verbo subiicimus*); for it is, as it has been said, like the touchstone, yea, it ought to be deemed most necessary to us; for that alone is true doctrine which is drawn from it."[71] The test of teachers is by the word and the Spirit, but the precise thing which is being questioned is whether or not the teachers have the Spirit by which they can rightly interpret the word.

We may observe that the difficulty Calvin faces in giving an adequate test of contemporary teachers and the circular kind of argument he employs in discussions of it are encountered again when Calvin explains how the authority of the original prophecies was secured. He likes to discuss this problem when commenting on those passages in which the prophets declare, "Thus saith the Lord." This declaration is always offered to secure authority for a prophecy. Of course, other passages in which God is not introduced as the speaker have no less authority. God is actually the speaker throughout. Nor is anyone who makes God the speaker doing so rightly. On the contrary, the argument is simply that when the prophet does so, he speaks the word of God and consequently is right. He gains more authority for his prophecy by doing this, although it must be emphasized that it does not give the prophecy more authority than it would have had anyway.[72]

Summary

The problem with which we have been dealing in this chapter is analogous to the problem involved in being certain of salvation. It is one thing, Calvin declares, to be certain of one's own salvation. It is another thing entirely to be certain of another's salvation.[73] A man is made certain of his own salvation by the witness of the Spirit of God. This is a meaningful and adequate way of explaining what happens to a person when he comes to faith. The knowledge involved is personal. It is not a matter subject to public test and demanding universal or even wide agreement. "As to others, we have no testimony, except from the outward efficacy of the Spirit; that is, in so far as the grace of God shews itself in them, so that we come to know it. There is, therefore, a great difference, because the assurance of faith remains inwardly shut up and does not extend itself to others."[74] This difficulty in knowing certainly the salvation of others is similar to the difficulty in ascertaining the validity of the teaching and interpretation of the Bible. For this wider knowledge Calvin employs the same correlation which he uses in relation to faith: word and Spirit. However, an obstacle appears which requires further handling, issuing in a completely circular argument in which it is difficult to fasten securely on any one point. The word must be taught and interpreted. For this the Spirit is necessary, but then the Spirit is tested by the word. Whenever Calvin introduces another possible criterion, he sooner or later qualifies it and works his way back to the word or the Spirit.

The fact is there can be no foolproof verification of authority outside of the word and the Spirit. To introduce one would be to introduce a human element, thereby piercing the defense behind which this Frenchman's theology securely developed.

PART III

Word

The Content and Character
of Knowledge

In the language of John Calvin "true and substantial wisdom" consists primarily of "the knowledge of God, and the knowledge of ourselves."[1] Theology is no more than the ordered presentation of the knowledge of God and self available to us. Calvin took pains to develop an explicit doctrine of authority in order that the material constituting his *Institutes*—and all his theological work for that matter—might be certain knowledge.

In the present day, in accordance with a growing philosophical interest in the analysis of language, writers are devoting more attention to the precise meaning of words. This pursuit has been of valuable assistance in historical studies since the modern period began. In the study of Calvin's principle of authority this search for precise meanings is essential. We have asked the relevant questions about the Spirit. In doing so we found that Calvin writes theology with two separable conceptions of the work of the Spirit. It is now our task to examine closely the other component element in the principle of authority—the word.

To ask questions about the meaning and use of the word is to ask questions about the meaning of the term "knowledge" as it is used by Calvin. As we have seen, for the Genevan Reformer the word is the only reliable source of knowledge in the Christian faith. By posing our questions to the term "knowledge" we will simultaneously be led to consider the material relating to the word of God. As we do this we will find, again, that Calvin operates with two separable conceptions of knowledge corresponding to the two conceptions of the work of the Spirit. In order to make this clear we will begin by investigating the content and character of knowledge. Chapter VII consists of a review of a few of the exegetical problems involved in assuming that the entire Bible is a source of knowledge. This corresponds to that section in Chapter V which deals with the difficulties Calvin faced in making the interpretative work of the Holy Spirit determinable in a public way. Chapter VIII, then, embodies a discussion of the response of the believer to the knowledge.

The Content of the Knowledge of Faith

Faith is seldom understood in terms of knowledge. For Calvin, however, faith is knowledge. In emphasizing the noetic aspect of faith Calvin was no innovator. He found this terminology in the Bible, particularly in the Gospel according to John, which was his favorite among the gospels, and I John, which he cited many times over. This which he found in the Bible, particularly in the writings of John, became the key category in his understanding of faith.

It was used to counter what Calvin considered to be perhaps the grossest evil in the Roman Catholic Church: the conception of implicit faith. "This notion," he declared, "has not only buried the true faith in oblivion, but has entirely destroyed it."[2] Against this he sets forth the axiom, "Faith consists not in ignorance, but in knowledge (*Non in ignoratione, sed in cognitione sita fides*)."[3]

The object of this knowledge of faith is quite concretely stated, but before we turn to it, it is well to observe the deliberate care with which Calvin approaches his own definition of it. We may with certain assurance say that in Calvin's own mind the entire contents of Book II and the first chapter of Book III were set forth as background material for the discussion of faith. The chapter in which faith is defined (III. ii) begins, "All these things will be easily understood when we have given a clearer definition of faith."[4] For itself, this statement could refer only to the previous chapter on the necessity of the work of the Spirit to confirm faith. That it refers not only to this but also to the whole of Book II is made clear when Calvin devotes the rest of this paragraph to a summary of the contents of that book in addition to the first chapter of Book III.[5]

The purpose of this summary statement is to proclaim that

Christ is the peculiar object of faith. Calvin even goes so far as to say that those who have said that God is the proper object of faith "rather mislead miserable souls by a vain speculation, than direct them to the proper mark."[6] The reason, of course, is that God himself is inaccessible. Christ as Mediator is necessary if we are to have God.[7] Christ is not thereby set over against God; rather, it is simply asserted that Christ is the means—the only means—by which we can believe in God.[8] Jesus Christ is the object of faith.

What does this mean? "This, then, is the true knowledge of Christ—to receive him as he is offered by the Father, that is, invested with his gospel; for, as he is appointed to be the object of our faith, so we cannot advance in the right way to him, without the guidance of the gospel."[9] There can be no doubt about what "gospel" signifies. "The gospel certainly opens to us those treasures of grace, without which Christ would profit us little."[10] Christ, then, who is the object of faith, is understood in terms of the gospel, which, in turn, is explained by reference to grace.

On the basis of this it is possible to move more closely to the precise content of the knowledge of faith. This knowledge is actually quite narrow. "For the apprehension of faith is not confined to our knowing that there is a God, but chiefly consists in our understanding what is his disposition towards us. For it is not of so much importance to us to know what he is in himself, as what he is willing to be to us. We find, therefore, that faith is a knowledge of the will of God respecting us, received from his word."[11] This disposition of God toward us, in which the knowledge of faith chiefly consists, has to do with the promises of grace and the covenant of mercy which Calvin found written into the Bible from the first page to the last. That the promises of God are the center as they are also the boundaries of the knowledge of faith could not be more clearly stated than in Calvin's "complete definition of faith": "It is a steady and certain knowledge of the Divine benevolence towards us, which, being founded on the truth of the gratuitous promise in Christ, is both revealed to our minds, and confirmed to our hearts, by the Holy Spirit."*

* III. ii. 7 (O.S. IV. 16.31–35) ; . . . *esse divinae erga nos benevolentiae firmam certamque cognitionem, quae gratuitae in Christo promis-*

Edward A. Dowey, Jr.[12] has carefully analyzed this definition
of faith, concluding[13] that the content of the knowledge of faith
can be stated in what may be considered the dual attribute of God
the Redeemer—gratuitous mercy. The knowledge of God the Redeemer, he asserts, centers in this single main theme of scripture.[14]
In order to show the centrality of this theme in Calvin's thought
he offers a striking number of examples in which Calvin uses such
terms as "gratuitous mercy," "gratuitous favor," "gratuitous
goodness," "mere good pleasure," and "gratuitous love."[15] In
his essay on the meaning of faith in Calvin's theology Peter Brunner also stresses the free goodness of God.* It is also this character
of God that Wilhelm Niesel emphasizes when he finds the key to
Calvin's theology in his Christocentrism.[16]

This knowledge of faith contains within itself the broad outlines of a more or less complete system of theology. It suggests a
doctrine of man as incapable of saving himself. It points to Jesus
Christ as the revelation of the divine will. Moreover, it proclaims
that man's ineptness is overcome and Christ's work made effective
through the work of the Holy Spirit. In short, one may say that
Calvin's doctrine of faith summarizes in a general way the major
themes discussed in Book II and Book III of the *Institutes.* It is
difficult to see how there could be any question at all about the
content of the knowledge of faith. Calvin's definition is clear and
concise. In faith one comes to know the "Divine benevolence"
and the "gratuitous promise in Christ." It is the gratuitous mercy
of God which constitutes the content of the knowledge of faith.

The Further Content of Knowledge

The content of the knowledge of faith, however, is by no means
the extent of the believer's knowledge. Dowey[17] compares the
knowledge of God the Creator with the knowledge of God the Redeemer, and he describes the content of both areas of knowledge.

*sionis veritate fundata, per Spiritum sanctum et revelatur mentibus nostris
et cordibus obsignatur.*

* *Vom Glauben bei Calvin,* pp. 62–91. The key descriptive words for
Brunner in explaining the knowledge of God in faith are *Barmherzigkeit*
and *Fülle.* See particularly pp. 62ff.

The two together constitute the *duplex cognitio Dei,* the twofold knowledge of God. This insight into the structure of the *Institutes,* although it deals with the knowledge available to one in the Christian faith, is not of concern to us here. What concerns us, rather, is to point out a certain contrast in the knowledge of faith and the knowledge granted to the believer in the Bible as a whole.

Philosophers of religion have sometimes been criticized for seeking to know too much. Calvin energetically echoed this criticism. Yet few men have ever lived whose thirst for a knowledge of their religion was more insatiable than that of John Calvin. The difference between Calvin and philosophers of religion rests in the estimation of man's ability to know. Calvin was more than modest in this respect, considering that men, in divine matters, are "blinder than moles." What knowledge a man has must be given to him. With this, Calvin's modesty came to a halt. His conception of the knowledge that has been given to men was as wide as the Bible itself.

Corresponding to his understanding of the work of the Holy Spirit in the writers of the Bible which issued in some form of the "dictation" theory, and corresponding to his conception of the Spirit's work in the believer confirming the Bible as a whole, Calvin held that everything which is stated in the Bible is knowledge for the believer. Not only is it available knowledge; it is also necessary knowledge. "Many are immediately satisfied with but moderate information, and as soon as they understand a portion of any subject, they reject every addition, and many too often settle down at the first elements, and their obstinacy prevents that complete knowledge which is necessary."[18] In his summary of the contents of I Corinthians Calvin claims that the epistle has many advantages. "It contains," he writes, "many special topics, the handling of which successively in their order, will show how necessary they are to be known."[19] He glories in the gift of knowledge promised in the Bible. "We hence see that the Prophet promises knowledge (*cognitionem*), so that they might be no longer alphabetarians; for these words, "Know ye Jehovah," point out the first elements of faith, or of celestial doctrine. . . . The meaning then is that all God's chosen people would be so endued with the gift of knowledge (*dono intelligentiae*), that they would no longer continue in the first elements."[20] Calvin thirsted for "all knowledge," but he understood by this "not a knowledge of all things," but rather "what is full and complete."[21] To his mind this could be found in the whole Bible and only there.

This means, of course, that the believer knows as much as the men who wrote the Bible, and in Calvin's mind this constituted a considerable range of knowledge. However God communicated with the patriarchs, "it is beyond a doubt that their minds were impressed with a firm assurance of the doctrine, so that they were persuaded and convinced that the information they had received came from God. . . . At length, that the truth might remain in the world in a continual course of instruction to all ages, he determined that the same oracles which he had deposited with the patriarchs should be committed to public records."[22] That which the patriarchs and all the others who were used in the composition of the scriptures were taught was not merely a knowledge of doctrines in the sense of broad themes. On the contrary, they were taught—and we can now know it as thoroughly as they did—a quite specific knowledge of matters of fact. They were not, for example, taught simply that God is the creator and that everything that has come into being is dependent for its existence on his creative word. Rather, they were taught—and we now have this teaching—a history of the creation. The purpose of such a history is to overthrow vain and worthless philosophies and to destroy the claims of fictitious deities,[23] but the lesson is secured by the specific content of the knowledge imparted. "The first thing specified in this history is the time, that by a continued series of years the faithful might arrive at the first original of the human race, and of all things."[24] If Calvin does not want to discuss this history fully he can simply refer his readers to the Bible. "It is better, as I have just advised the reader, to seek for fuller information on this subject from Moses, and others who have faithfully and diligently recorded the history of the world (*mundi historiam*)."[25] The content of this knowledge is so concrete that Calvin can, on the basis of the second chapter of Genesis, draw up a map locating the beginning of human life.[26] There is no problem involved in explaining how Moses could know these things that had happened so long before his own time, or for that matter how he could know as clearly and concretely things that happened long after his death. He was only "the instrument of the Holy Spirit for the publication of those things which it was of importance for all men to know."[27]

It goes without saying that Calvin was not different from his contemporaries or his predecessors in understanding the content of the scripture in this way. Galileo was forced to recant his scientific discoveries because they countered the express teaching of scripture. Calvin did not bring forth a new exegesis of the miracle of Gibeon. He merely bequeathed to the traditional understanding the flavor of his own style with its uncompromising finality: "The question how the sun stood in Gibeon, is no less unseasonably raised by some than unskilfully explained by others."[28] He does not bother himself with how many hours it stood still, but he will have nothing to do with the attempt to explain it away by claiming that the battle took place on the longest day of the year. "In short," he concludes, "the sun, which was already declining to the west, is kept from setting."[29]

Most theologians in Calvin's day—including, of course, his counterpart in Germany, Martin Luther—had the same view. Calvin *was* like his contemporaries. The reason, however, for mentioning this fact at this point is to indicate that Calvin *had* to explain scripture this way. He operated on the basis of a doctrine of authority which demanded it. As we have seen, he conceived the Bible to have no human admixtures in it. The way in which he correlated word and Spirit left no room for a principle of distinction within the scripture. If, on occasion, he rose above this literalism and wrote theology in a way that did not demand a literalistic view of the scripture, it was not because he rejected what he upheld in so many other places but rather because he could do the one without violating the other.

This conception of the Bible was naturally conducive to the positivistic use of the scriptures. In Chapter IV we observed in passing that the positivistic use of the scripture was not unusual for Calvin, and we cited his proof of the divinity of the Holy Spirit by putting together in syllogistic form verses of scripture from different parts of the Bible and then drawing the certain conclusion. This was only one way in which he used scripture to prove a point. More often it was not necessary for him to relate passages. In Psalm 110 the use of the word *chohen* was sufficient proof to Calvin that David is speaking of Christ. The Jews try to undermine the prediction by translating the word "prince," and although Calvin acknowledges that the word can stand for one of noble descent, he considers the Jewish translation "feeble and frivolous." "Would it have been saying anything to the honour of Christ," he argues, "for David merely to give him the title of a chief, which is inferior to that of royal dignity?"[30]

In a similar way Calvin argues that the resurrection is a fact because the linen clothes were left behind, and it is unlikely that men would have stripped the body naked in order to move it to another place.[31] Calvin can also assure his readers of the resurrection by virtue of the methodical way in which Christ's body was buried and watched carefully and the inability of men to find the body after the resurrection. "Whence we may gather the certainty of the resurrection," he concludes.[32] That God's mercy is greater than his wrath can be shown by pointing out in scripture that his mercy extends to a thousand generations whereas his wrath extends only to the fourth generation.[33]

At numerous points Calvin proves his point by the total force of multiple quotations from scripture. In this way he substantiates a view of human responsibility for sin that would otherwise be difficult to explain: "I deny, then, that sin is the less criminal, because it is necessary; I deny also the other consequence, which they infer, that it is avoidable because it is voluntary."[34] This is also the proof of the humanity of Jesus: "As the Holy Spirit has on so many occasions, by so many instruments, and with such great diligence and simplicity, declared a fact by no means abstruse in itself, who could have supposed that any mortals would have such consummate impudence as to dare to obscure it with subtilties?"[35] It is characteristic of Calvin to write, "Let us give the reader a summary of the doctrine and prove it by a few very clear testimonies of Scripture."[36]

Dual Bases for Theological Themes

A good many of the doctrines dealt with in the *Institutes* were submitted to a treatment from two aspects. Calvin was even ready to substantiate a point of view by some means of proof from scripture, but he also sought out, where possible, the relation of a doctrine to the central doctrine of faith. He was eminently a practical theologian. He wrote theology to be helpful, to edify—and to him this meant relating the discussion to some facet of the doctrine of faith where possible. On the other hand, since he considered everything in the scripture to be not only edifying but quite necessary to be known, a relation to the doctrine of faith was not a criterion for entering upon a discussion of any particular doctrine.

Calvin's exposition of the doctrine of the providence of God is a case in point. The main discussion is in Chapter XVI of Book I, "God's preservation and Support of the World by His Power and His Government of Every part of It by His Providence." In this chapter Calvin is most interested in describing "the providence of God, as it is taught in scripture."[37] The orderly arrangement of numerous passages of scripture relating to providence is more than sufficient to make the case and to create assurance of the doctrine in the heart of the believer. His rebuff to those who want to attribute to God the principle of motion and yet hold that things are governed by the laws of nature is characteristic of the treatment of other problems in this chapter:

> But as it would be tedious to collect all the reasons for rejecting this error, let us be content with the authority of God himself. In the law and in the prophets he frequently declares, that whenever he moistens the earth with dew or with rain, he affords a testimony of his favour; and that, on the contrary, when, at his command, heaven becomes hard as iron, when the crops of corn are blasted and otherwise destroyed, and when showers of hail and storms molest the fields, he gives a proof of his certain and special vengeance. If we believe these things, it is certain (*certum est*) that not a drop of rain falls but at the express command of God.[38]

In the next chapter ("The Proper Application of This Doctrine to Render It Useful to Us"), when Calvin meets the common ob-

jection to this doctrine, he again reverts to the positivistic use of
scripture. If someone says, "Why exercise oneself if all is determined by God?" the Reformer retorts that the proper human
response is to search the scriptures to find what is pleasing to God.[39]
On the other hand, in that chapter Calvin begins by showing that
"the Scripture doctrine of the Divine ordination of all things . . .
tends to show the care of God for the whole human race."[40]
Moreover, in this chapter the tone of Calvin's writing approaches
more nearly to that of ecstasy than at any other point in the *Institutes*. This occurs where he begins by declaring, "When this
light of Divine providence has once shined on a pious man, he is
relieved and delivered not only from the extreme anxiety and
dread with which he was previously oppressed, but also from all
care."[41] When Calvin speaks of the care of God for all men he
certainly relates providence to mercy, and when he extols that
absolute dependence of a man on God which frees him from all
care one is led to think of the gratuitous quality of that mercy.
The doctrine of providence is a theological theme with two parallel sources.

This is true of many other discussions in the *Institutes*, sometimes unexpectedly. One would think, for example, that when our
author embarks on a discussion of the angels he has taken on a
subject which can fill a number of folio pages only by the quotation and analysis of scripture verses. This is the way he begins.
First he urges his readers to observe the "rule of modesty and so-
briety; which is, not to speak, or think, or even desire to know,
concerning obscure subjects, any thing beyond the information
given us in the Divine word."[42] Then he searches the Bible for all
of the statements about angels in order to set forth the extent of
our knowledge of angels. Some points are quite clear; on others
he can only say that the scripture is inconclusive. After he has
summarized what can be known about angels without speculating
(i.e., what is clearly stated in the Bible), he then relates that
knowledge to the knowledge of faith. Because there are so many
dangers that face us and because we are so weak, lest we fall into
despair, God promises not only to care for us himself but also to
send us "life-guards."[43]

There are two sources for most of the doctrines in the other three books of the *Institutes* as well. In the discussion of free will in Book II Calvin tries to say only what the scripture says and declares that we must not impose our own laws on God.[44] We must also note, however, that the denial of free will is necessary to the doctrine of faith insofar as the affirmation of free will would imply that man can at least cooperate in his own salvation. If the latter were possible, the mercy of God would be somewhat maimed and the gratuitous character of it would be unnecessary. Calvin, on the contrary, maintains that it is vain for us to claim ability to fulfill God's law. "The grace of the Legislator is both necessary for us, and promised to us."[45] In the same Book the office of Christ as Redeemer is proved in a matter-of-fact way by citing 49 references to the scriptures in less than seven short pages.[46] Most of these are quoted after saying, "Now, that Christ by his obedience has really procured and merited grace from the Father for us, is certainly and justly concluded from various passages of Scripture."[47] However, we must also remember that Christ as Redeemer is the essence of the kerygma in its most general statement and that Calvin put this conviction into the very center of his definition of faith.

On the one hand, the doctrine of election is a corollary of the doctrine of faith, but, on the other hand, the knowledge is expanded considerably and given much more detail by the collection of relevant verses of scripture. Justification by faith is, one may say, in the definition of faith itself, but Calvin's discussion of it is strongly flavored by the copious quotation of proof texts quoted in a characteristic proof text fashion. He defines a Church by relating it integrally to the doctrine of faith ("Wherever we find the word of God purely preached and heard, and the sacraments administered according to the institution of Christ"),[48] but his discussion of it makes use of the scripture in the way we have noted above. Even sacraments which are actually the proclamation of the word of gratuitous mercy are determined and defended on the basis of a positivistic use of scripture. Other doctrines could be mentioned, but perhaps this sampling of two discussions from each of the four books in the *Institutes* will serve to show Calvin's common practice of giving double foundations for various theological themes.

There is an actual difference in these two bases. The one calls for understandings; the other calls for recognition and submission. The one moves into relations with other doctrines; the other is finished with the bare statement of it. In the context of the second, Calvin can be seen as a man in relentless pursuit of the correct knowledge which is incumbent on every believer. He will be seen as one given more to repristination than his counterpart in Germany. In this office he will set forth the outlines for a government of the Church derived from the government of the Church in the New Testament, and he will ban the use of musical instruments in worship.* In the same vein and under the same influence he will become most sternly legalistic and disciplinary in his view of the Christian life and the maintenance of order in the Church. The dual bases of theological themes are distinct, but Calvin himself would never have considered separating them. Both bases were derived ultimately from the same principle of authority: the correlation of word and Spirit.

The Character of Knowledge

Certain conclusions concerning the character of knowledge in John Calvin's theology could easily be drawn from the material already discussed. The task before us now is simply to order these implications and point out their significance.

For one thing, the knowledge of faith is more a persuasion

---

* This is a curiosity in Calvin as it is also a curiosity in our own day among the Churches of Christ. The Churches of Christ do not allow musical instruments because they are not mentioned in the worship of the New Testament Church. Calvin opposed them for two reasons: first, "musical instruments were among the legal ceremonies which Christ at His coming abolished" [Com. Ex. 15:20 (C.O. 24.162)]. The second reason was based on Paul's prohibition of speaking in unknown tongues: "We are not, indeed, forbidden to use, in private, musical instruments, but they are banished out of the churches by the plain command of the Holy Spirit, when Paul, in I Cor. 14:13, lays it down as an invariable rule, that we must praise God, and pray to him only in a known tongue" [Com. Ps. 71:22 (C.O. 31.662)].

than a cognition. Certainly Calvin uses the Latin word *cognitio* for the knowledge of faith, but he explains it in such a way that it is clearly not cognitive in the same way other matters are said to be cognitive in the present day.

> When we call it knowledge (*cognitionem*), we intend not such a comprehension (*comprehensionem*) as men commonly have of those things which fall under the notice of their senses. For it is so superior, that the human mind must exceed and rise above itself, in order to attain to it. Nor does the mind which attains it comprehend (*assequitur*) what it perceives (*sentit*), but being persuaded (*persuasum*) of that which it cannot comprehend (*capit*), it understands more by the certainty of this persuasion (*plus ipsa persuasionis certitudine*), than it would comprehend of any human object by the exercise of its natural capacity.[49]

Believers, Calvin agrees with John, have a certain knowledge that they are sons of God, "but they are rather confirmed by a persuasion of the veracity of God, than taught by any demonstration of reason."[50]

It is almost as if Calvin himself denied the cognitive character of the *cognitio fidei*, the knowledge of faith. This suspicion is further borne out by the fact that he uses the language of the heart in describing it. "The seat of faith is not in the head (*in cerebro*), but in the heart (*in corde*). Yet I would not contend about the part of the body in which faith is located: but as the word *heart* is often taken for a serious and sincere feeling (*serio et sincero affectu*), I would say that faith is a firm and effectual confidence (*firmam esse et efficacem fiduciam*), and not a bare notion only (*non nudam tantum notionem*)."[51] It is remarkable how passages in the chapter on faith are literally saturated with such terms as "persuasion," "pious affections," "firmly seals within them," "impression of the Spirit," "heart," "delight," and "sure and certain experience."[52] In the commentary on Ezekiel he says that the people "really felt him to be God, because he stood firm to his promises."[53] This noncognitive—or more than cognitive—character of the knowledge of faith is clear when Calvin indicates that it "consists more in certainty than in comprehension."[54]

In contrast with this, the full range of knowledge available in the Bible as a whole is more truly cognitive, as may be seen from the matter-of-fact way in which Calvin makes use of it. When the Bible is taken in this way it is understood to communicate to its readers the state of the affairs about which it speaks. When, for example, someone rebuffs Calvin's denial of free will by saying that if this were the case there would be no sense in exhorting men to be different from what they are, Calvin closes the case by calling attention to the fact that in the scriptures we are commanded to exhort.[55] This datum is sufficient to counter all human reasoning as far as Calvin is concerned. Because he considered the biblical material as data, he was entirely consistent in considering as monstrous the error of the crowd in John 12:29 when it mistook the clear words of God, "This is my beloved Son," for thunder.[56]

It should be remembered, on the other hand, that when Calvin writes in Book I about that work of the Spirit in confirming the scriptures in the believer, he uses much the same kind of language as he uses in the discussion of faith. This, too, is accomplished by the internal work of the Holy Spirit. This, too, is beyond the powers of the human reason to confirm. This, too, is a persuasion. In Chapter V we observed some of the problems Calvin faced in the complete development of this principle, but that he used a comparable language is not to be denied. Despite this, however, there is a difference in the significance of the language. In the one case the internal persuasion is that God is gratuitous mercy. In the other a man is persuaded that the Bible is the work of the Holy Spirit. The knowledge content of the one must always remain an inner persuasion; it can never be separated from this subjective character. With the other the persuasion confirms something which in turn opens up for the believer an almost infinite range of data which itself is not at all related to the internal persuasion.

This brings us to a second contrast in the character of knowledge in Calvin's theology. The knowledge of faith is personal whereas the wider knowledge is objective and informational. The personal character of the knowledge of faith is underlined in Calvin's definition by the inclusion of *erga nos*—it is a persuasion of the divine benevolence *toward us.* The moment of faith's cognition—if we may continue to use that word—is the moment of being saved. Faith is, to be sure, a knowledge of something that God has done in Christ quite outside of men, but it is more. It is the knowledge that what God has done in Christ is done *erga nos,* or better, *erga me.* "No man is truly a believer, unless he be firmly persuaded, that God is a propitious and benevolent Father to him,"[57] and this "to him" must be repeated. One does not depend on the promises of the divine benevolence but on "the promises of the Divine benevolence to him."[58] "The principal hinge on which faith turns is this—that we must not consider the promises of mercy, which the Lord offers, as true only to others, and not to ourselves; but rather make them our own, by embracing them in our hearts."[59] Even the heathens could gather some vague notion of the immortality of the soul, but it would be impossible for any one of them to have real assurance of it or to speak of it as a thing known "to him." This is possible only to believers on the basis of the word and the Spirit.

> This knowledge is not merely of a general kind, as though believers were merely in a general way persuaded, that the children of God will be in a better condition after death, and had no assurance as to themselves individually, for of how very little service this would be for affording a consolation, so difficult of attainment! On the contrary, every one must have a knowledge peculiar to himself (*de se particularem scientiam*), for this, and this only, can animate me to meet death with cheerfulness—if I am fully persuaded, that I am departing to a better life.[60]

Notice how Calvin shifts at the end of this statement from the third person to the first person. It is as though he were driven to this by virtue of the intensely personal character of this knowledge.

There are at least two correlates to this. For one thing, the knowledge of God's gratuitous mercy is always accompanied in the believer by a new self-understanding. We have seen how Calvin considers the knowledge of God and the knowledge of self to be related in theology. This relation is most clearly seen in the act of faith. The free goodness of God becomes a conviction in the heart of a man only as he is himself searched to the quick and surrenders every fragment of his human boasting. It is when men are "humbled by a true knowledge of themselves" that "they flee to the grace of Christ."[61]

The other correlate is in part derived from the first. Along with the knowledge of faith comes a participation in Christ. Divested of himself, a man is made one with Christ. "For this is our trust, this is our glory, and the only anchor of our salvation, That Christ the Son of God is ours, and that we are likewise, in him, sons of God and heirs of the celestial kingdom; being called, not for our worthiness, but by the Divine goodness, to the hope of eternal felicity."[62] When Calvin speaks of receiving Christ in faith he does not mean that he is received only in the understanding (*intelligentia*) or the imagination (*imaginatione*), nor does he mean that in faith one rests in mere contemplation and simple knowledge (*nuda notitia*). On the contrary, the reception issues in "a real participation of him."[63] Then he adds, "And, in fact, I see not how any man can attain a solid confidence that he has redemption and righteousness in the cross of Christ, and life in his death, unless he first has a real communion with Christ himself (*nisi vera Christi ipsius communione in primis fretus*); for those blessings would never be imparted to us, if Christ did not first make himself ours (*nisi se prius nostrum Christus faceret*)."[64]

Opposed to this, the knowledge derived from a literalistic use of the scriptures is objective and informational in character. The *erga nos* is not found in Calvin's doctrine of the scripture, nor is it mentioned in the chapter on the work of the Spirit in confirming the scripture. No new self-understanding is involved in believing in the divine source of scripture. Certainly one may be taught his depraved condition in the pages of the Bible, but such a self-understanding is not a correlate to the belief in scripture in a way comparable to what we saw in the act of faith. Finally, it is not necessary or even coherent to speak of the believer's communion with Christ in the discussion of the scriptures.

One may speak of the wider knowledge as didactic and of the knowledge of faith as kerygmatic. Calvin's definition of faith embodies the main elements of what we have come to call in recent years the kerygma of the early Church. The word of grace, the free forgiveness of sin, justification by faith alone, Christ—this was the proclamation of the early Church as it was also the watchword of the Reformation. The very content of the knowledge demanded that it be communicated through preaching. Calvin sensed this, and in a large measure he complied. He became primarily didactic, however, when he turned to the positivistic use of the scripture. Then he was interested in passing on information to those who listened to him or read his words.[65] It is interesting to note how Calvin is moved to speak of the scripture's "instruction" at the *locus classicus* for the dictation theory of inspiration.[66]

In the last place—if we may borrow the language of Paul Tillich—the knowledge of faith may be called theonomous, and the wider knowledge heteronomous. Tillich uses these terms mainly for the analysis of whole cultures, but they are equally applicable as descriptive terms for the character of knowledge. " 'Theonomy,' " Tillich writes, "has been defined as a culture in which the ultimate meaning of existence shines through all finite forms of thought and action."[67] "Heteronomy," on the other hand, he defines as "the attempt of a religion to dominate autonomous cultural creativity from the outside."[68] When Calvin describes faith, he makes it clear that the knowledge involved in it illumines the ultimate meaning of one's life in a way that anything finite could not possibly do. When he uses the Bible as the source of information and objective instruction, what he says stands over against a man and dominates him from the outside. The most appropriate response to the former is *fiducia*—trust; the most appropriate response to the latter is *obedientia*—unquestioning obedience. The more complete discussion of this response will be the subject of our interest in Chapter VIII.

Peculiarities
in Calvin's Exegesis

Any discussion of Calvin's work as an exegete should begin with the acknowledgment that he possessed in a way remarkable for his age many of the tools of his trade. He was learned in both biblical languages, and he had an amazing command of the scriptures. Consonant with his kinship to the humanists he was interested in recovering the original meaning of the authors, and he exercised a considerable learning and ability in pursuit of the relatively new science of historical exegesis. Although he had a weakness for typology, he disclaimed allegory and was constantly seeking out the natural meaning of the text on the basis of the original sources. Certainly his exegesis was uneven in this respect, and he made numerous historical errors, but his commentaries are still seriously studied. Some scholars consider Calvin to have been one of the greatest of all exegetes.

The purpose of this chapter is not at all to create doubt about Calvin's ability as an interpreter of scripture. One must stand in profound admiration of the power and scope of this exegetical mind. The purpose, as the chapter title indicates, is to focus on certain peculiarities in Calvin's exegesis which are apparently prompted by his conviction that the entire Bible is the work of the Holy Spirit and consequently an internally consistent unity. For one who holds such a conviction an explicit norm of interpretation external to the Bible itself is unthinkable, and it is noteworthy that Calvin does not articulate one. If we are thoroughly to assess Calvin's principle of authority, we must carefully observe the ways in which he treats those passages of scripture which raise questions about the unity of the Bible.

Flexible Hermeneutical Guides

In his exegesis Calvin made use of several hermeneutical guides in locating the proper meaning of biblical texts. The two which he most often used were the principle of accommodation and the figure of speech, synecdoche. The principle of accommodation* calls attention to the fact that in the Bible God "lisps," as it were, to us. The Holy Spirit uses language that is not precisely proper to the subject being discussed but which nevertheless is used out of condescension to the human capacity. We will shortly have cause to see this principle in action in relation to an aspect of Calvin's doctrine of God. It is sufficient here to observe a curiosity about the use of the doctrine. Ostensibly the cause of God's lisping to us is in order that we may understand what we could not understand were the matter stated in more proper language. It is common for Calvin to write that a passage of the Bible is stated in such a way "in accommodation to the imperfection of the human understanding."[1] The difficulty with this, however, is that in order for a man to know what the passage of scripture really means, one must point out to him that the language has been accommodated and that its significance is actually something quite different from what the words themselves would indicate.

A similar difficulty prevails in the use of synecdoche as a means of getting at the meaning of a text. Calvin claims that this figure has been consistently used in the Ten Commandments. As he approaches the discussion of these commandments in the *Institutes* he devotes a paragraph to the mode of interpreting the commandments in order to avoid seeing too little or too much in them.[2] He claims that the figure, synecdoche, is conspicuous in all the commandments. In the French version of the *Institutes* of 1541 he defined synecdoche at this point as a figure of speech in which "a part is expressed instead of the whole."[3] On the basis of this he finds it possible to considerably expand the scope of the commandments in two directions. For one thing, he understands the object of a command to be the genus of a species, as when he says that the prohibition of killing means that "we should not unjustly do violence to any one."[4] In the other direction, he infers the

* See above, pp. 13–14.

positive from the negative: "There is a manifest synecdoche in this Commandment (the third); for in order that God may procure for His name its due reverence, He forbids its being taken in vain, especially in oaths. Whence we infer on the other hand an affirmative commandment, that every oath should be a testimony of true piety, whereby the majesty of God Himself should obtain its proper glory."[5]

Most often Calvin uses synecdoche as a figure in which the part is expressed instead of the whole. It helps him to explain why Joshua is not really omitted when Moses announces that only Caleb will live to enter the promised land,[6] and it solves a host of other problems.[7] Occasionally, however, he understands the figure in exactly the opposite way, as stating the whole when only a part is meant. In this way he explains a divergency in the gospels about the number of women at the tomb. It may have been that "Matthew, by synecdoche, . . . extended to all what was peculiar to one of their number."[8] In another place, "Matthew and Mark, by synecdoche, attribute to the robbers what was done only by one of them, as is evident from Luke."[9] This use of synecdoche is less common than the other, but it does occur with some degree of frequency.[10] The difficulty with this figure is obvious. First, there is no key given for determining when the figure is used, and then there is no way of clearly determining which meaning the figure is to have in any one place.

Another figure—more sparingly used—is *hysteron proteron*, a Greek term which means the first is put last. Calvin employs it to excuse Jacob of fraud toward his father-in-law by noting that Moses subsequently relates that Jacob did nothing without first being commanded by God.[11] It also allows him to put the death of Isaac in its "proper order."[12] With this figure, as with the others, there is no key for determining when it is used.

Calvin often interprets passages which are similar in structure and significance in directly opposite ways. Sometimes acts of prophetic symbolism are understood literally while at other times they are not. Calvin thought Ezekiel really ate the scroll in 3:1–2,[13] but he did not really lie on his side for over a year.[14] The saying after one of the Egyptian plagues, "All the cattle died," is a "comprehensive expression" (*synecdochica est locuutio*),[15] but when "all" the people answer Moses and the elders in Exodus 19:8 we must understand that no one dissented even by silence.[16] In the exposition of the Sermon on the Mount, Calvin explains away a reward for fastings and puts fasting in a category different from prayer and alms.[17] Also it is interesting how Calvin is flexible on the repentance which the Bible associates with baptism, and inflexible on the examination which is supposed to take place before communion. Infants may be baptized into a future repentance,[18] but children may not take communion because they are not old enough to stand a mature examination.[19]

In all of these places as well as in others Calvin interprets with no consistent key for determining which statements should be taken for what they say and which statements should be freely interpreted. As a matter of fact, it would have been quite impossible for Calvin to give a predetermined pattern for exegesis which one might consistently follow. Calvin's consistency was in another area altogether. That had to do with the conclusion of all exegesis. We must remember that the exegete begins with a conviction about the divine authorship of the scriptures—a conviction which has been divinely imparted to him. Thus it is a foregone conclusion that all exegesis must uphold the divinity and, therefore, the unity and perfection of scripture. In this respect Calvin was remarkably consistent. If this consistency meant that at times he had to depart from what seems to the contemporary reader the natural meaning of the text, it can only be countered that to Calvin the natural meaning of a text is that which upholds the divine authorship of scripture. Because of this, Calvin as an exegete was free to read into a passage whatever might be necessary in order to arrive at the foregone conclusion. Nonetheless, since Calvin was a man, subject to the frailties which he himself so graphically described, these additions to the Bible were sometimes flavored by his own personal predispositions toward the subject at hand.

Maintaining the Unity and Perfection of Scripture

It was, of course, unthinkable to Calvin that a prophetic prediction should not be fulfilled. He applies most prophecies to the kingdom of Christ, but with varying degrees of difficulty. Sometimes, as with Isaiah's prediction of the return from captivity, the actual fulfillment is considered only "a dark foreshadowing of the deliverance" in Christ.[20] This is all the more clear by the fact that the return was not all that the prophets indicated it would be.[21] At other times, it is clear that prophecies could not have referred to pre-Christian history because they were not fulfilled then; and if the coming of Christ does not seem appropriate to the language of the prophet, then the reference must be to something that will happen at the end of history.[22] Hosea apparently predicts the restoration of the northern tribes, but this is not really the case because the northern tribes were not, in fact, restored.[23] Of Obadiah's prophecy Calvin writes, "Now it is certain that this prophecy [that the Jews would possess the whole land of Palestine] has never been completed." Therefore it "unquestionably" refers to the kingdom of Christ.[24]

Calvin employs a number of devices in upholding the unity of the scriptures. Occasionally, when he encounters different accounts of the same narrative he decides that the full story is the sum of all the parts. If Matthew and Mark indicate that the head of Christ was anointed and John says the feet were anointed, the conclusion is that "the whole body of Christ, down to the feet, was anointed."[25] Many Old Testament scholars think the conflicting attitudes toward the establishment of the monarchy in Israel indicate separate traditions and separate authors. Calvin, however, saw no conflict at all. The monarchy was the design of God, but because the people were too hasty in setting it up it is also attributed to their sin.[26]

This method of reconciling divergencies at times required clarifying additions to the text. Mark and Luke indicate that one blind man was healed as Jesus entered Jericho. Matthew says that two were healed as he left the city. Calvin concludes that there were in fact two. The gospel writers were not always concerned with details, he claims, and adds that one of the blind men encouraged the other to implore Jesus.[27] In the same way Calvin reconciles the divergent accounts of the distribution of the promised land among the Hebrew tribes. One account says it was done by Joshua, Eleazar, and the princes, another that it was determined by lots. The conclusion: Lots determined the general positions of tribes and then the leaders determined the sizes according to the rules of equity.[28]

The problems of chronology in the Pentateuch were one of the main contributing factors in the formation of the documentary hypothesis in Old Testament criticism. For Calvin, however, there are no problems. It is well known that Moses did not always place events in their proper order,[29] and the various modes of speaking must be considered. The author may have taken into account the beginning of a period as well as its end, he may have left out a detail which Calvin can supply, or he may have overlooked a smaller sum since he was dealing with a larger one.[30]

A similar means employed by Calvin is to take the most inclusive account as the full story. This is his most useful method in reconciling apparent differences in the accounts of the resurrection appearances.[31] In the same way he finds agreement in the two speeches of Joshua which, he declares, are accounts of the same speech, the latter explaining and interpreting the former.[32] He also reconciles the divergent accounts of the withering of the fig tree in Matthew and Mark,[33] and explains how one account could say that Noah took animals by twos, and another by sevens.[34]

Just as he uses the more complete of two narratives to explain the other, he uses one part of the Bible to explain other parts. This is based on the well-known principle that the Bible is its own interpreter, and we saw earlier* how Calvin used Paul in order to arrive at the true meaning of James. In the same way he explains away positive references to works,[35] the denial of a second repentance in Hebrews,[36] and the prohibition of swearing.[37] If a New Testament writer quotes from the Old Testament, then the understanding of that passage is unquestionably what the New Testament writer makes it out to be.†

This practice, as we saw in the case of the interpretation of justification by works in James, often calls for an interpretative addition to the text. In the case of the book of James, one had to

---

* Above, pp. 60–61.
† Cf. Com. Ps. 68:18 (C.O. 31.628); Com. Ps. 69:21 (C.O. 31.646). In Com. Dt. 32:35 (C.O. 25.373) Calvin calls attention to the fact that this statement is quoted to different purposes and meanings in Rom. 12:19 and Heb. 10:30, but he claims that both places give a true interpretation.

understand that James did not use the word "justification" in the
same way Paul did. Other cases follow the same line. Old Testament scholars have puzzled over the denial by some of the eighth-
and seventh-century prophets that God did not command sacrifices
in the wilderness. Calvin claims that when Jeremiah made this
denial he only intended to say that "God regards not sacrifices in
themselves."[38] Again in the Old Testament, one of the growing
conflicts in Hebrew religion from the time of the exile on was that
between universalism and particularism. Calvin, however, takes
Joel's prediction that no aliens will pass through Jerusalem to be
a promise that God will be the protector of his Church against her
enemies.[39] With statements bordering on universalism like "God
wishes all men to be saved" in I Timothy 1:4 Calvin explains that
the "all" refers to all classes and ranks of men rather than to all
men, so that there is no contradiction of the doctrine of election.[40]
A host of other difficulties is escaped in the same way when Calvin
gives some unexpected twist to a word, or enlightens his reader on
the unexpressed intention of the writer of the passage in question.[41]

The unity of scripture was a conclusion Calvin had to uphold.
The strength of his conviction and not just the promptings of his
opponents compelled him to deal thoroughly with every conceivable threat to this unity which his wide knowledge of the Bible
suggested to him. The irony of his work, however, is that in his
determined effort to maintain the divine authorship of the scripture at every point he was driven to a form of exegesis in which
the literal meaning of the text was often denied and in which it
became the task of the exegete to add, subtract, or create, depending on the nature of the case.

Calvin's Program of Demythologization

A current debate which has warmed the theological pot to a
vigorous boiling has been that which centers around the name of
Rudolph Bultmann. Central to this debate has been Bultmann's
program of demythologizing the New Testament. Bultmann conceives that the New Testament was written out of the background
of a prescientific world view, and he claims that all of the myth
associated with this world view must be reinterpreted in terms of

our modern scientific world view if contemporary men are to understand what the gospel is all about. The strength of Bultmann's argument is partly witnessed by the fact that most theologians have a more or less studied opinion about his program. He has been loudly hailed, and he has been roundly criticized. One strong critic, Julius Schniewind, it is interesting to note, concedes this much: "Bultmann's desire to emancipate the gospel message from mythology is something which he shares with every preacher who is worth his salt."[42]

According to Schniewind's criterion, John Calvin as a teacher and preacher was at least to some extent worth his salt. Calvin himself had a program of demythologization. Of course, most of the myth with which contemporary men are concerned was maintained rather literally by the Genevan preacher, but in one area he consistently and thoroughly followed the way of demythologization. That was in his doctrine of God. We are going to look at this emphasis now because it illuminates another difficulty Calvin faced in his exegetical work.

Calvin's conception of God was that God is in himself out of relation with the world. He is immutable and wholly other in the sense that everything carnal and earthly is utterly inappropriate in talking about him. "God, we know, is subject to no passions; and we know that no change takes place in him."[43] When Calvin interprets the prayer of Christ in Gethsemane, it is telling that he prefers to say—as easily as possible—that this was not a premeditated prayer of Christ and that he momentarily gave way to the darkness of distressing anxiety rather than to say that the implication that God could change his will was a possibility. "All things are possible to thee," says Jesus. Calvin answers, "But it would be improper to extend the power of God so far as to lessen his truth, by making him liable to variety and change."[44]

With this conviction Calvin added to his already burdened shoulders a not inconsiderable task. It is characteristic of the Bible, especially the Old Testament, to speak freely of God in human terms. Calvin, however, approached his task armed with figures of speech to which he had recourse in his encounter with the biblical language. Two may especially be mentioned. The one was hypotyposis.[45] This is a figure by which a thing is described so vividly that it seems to stand before one's eyes, tangible and visible rather than immaterial. The other figure was anthropopatheia, which Calvin defined in the margin of his commentary on the Psalms: "It occurs when we attribute to God human passions, attachments and modes of life."[46] Although Calvin seldom referred to these figures by name, he probably had them in mind. One or the other or both of them cover every instance of his demythologizing the language about God in the Bible. Most often, he had recourse to the principle of accommodation; it may justly be said this was the main use he made of this dominant principle.

Calvin simply could not accept biblical language referring to God's activity. His explanation of God's activity in helping Adam and Eve when the eyes of that pair were opened and they were ashamed of their nakedness is remarkable:

> Moses here, in a homely style, declares that the Lord had undertaken the labour of making garments of skins for Adam and his wife. It is not indeed proper so to understand his words, as if God had been a furrier, or a servant to sew clothes. Now, it is not credible that skins should have been presented to them by chance; but, since animals had before been destined for their use, being now impelled by a new necessity, they put some to death, in order to cover themselves with their skins, having been divinely directed to adopt this counsel; therefore Moses calls God the Author of it.[47]

The point, however, is that Moses did not call God the "Author" of this activity in the way Calvin wants it; the author of the narrative relates that God himself made garments of skins for Adam and Eve. This, according to the narrative, is more than an order of creation. But it is not a divine direction. It is, rather, an activity of God.

It is also interesting to observe Calvin's treatment of Jacob's wrestling with an angel which, Calvin claims, must be understood as God himself. The interpretation, however, is of such a nature that this wrestling is made out to be nothing different from the struggle every man faces in the life of faith. The purpose of the story is "to teach us that our faith is tried by him; and whenever we are tempted, our business is truly with him."[48] In the same way

Calvin must explain away why Moses was commanded to remove his shoes before the burning bush "lest, in our gross imaginations, we should, as it were, draw down God from heaven, and affix him to places on earth; and, also, lest we should account that sanctity perpetual which is only temporary." He decides that Moses was made to take off his shoes "as a preparation to listen with greater reverence to God." "For since the nature of God is spiritual, it is not allowable to imagine respecting him anything earthly or gross; nor does his immensity permit of his being confined to place."[49] The text indicates that the place on which Moses was standing was holy ground, but Calvin cannot allow that because it implies God's involvement in the gross and earthly.

It can easily be seen, then, how Calvin cannot allow those passages to stand which attribute to God any human activities or senses. Whenever he comes to a verse which attributes such things to God, he takes pains to make unmistakably clear that the language is improper and that the author doesn't really mean what he says, but that the Holy Spirit is here accommodating his language to our low capacities. Thus he treats all references to God's remembering,[50] resting,[51] repenting,[52] returning,[53] sleeping,[54] yearning,[55] smelling,[56] seeing,[57] wondering,[58] laughing,[59] speaking,[60] and using spears and bucklers.[61] In all these instances he tells what the particular activity or sensation attributed to God really means, and he does so in each case in such a way as to protect the immutability and wholly otherness of God.

The reader of Calvin may be led to think that God is so wholly other that he has no relationship at all with men, and even that he has never had relationship with them in the past. The relationship has always occurred through Christ. This is perhaps the main reason Calvin is so thorough in reading Christ into the Old Testament, and perhaps it is the main strength in the title "Mediator." Calvin is convinced that Jehovah (Yahweh), the name for God in the Old Testament, is "attributed to the presiding Angel, who was undoubtedly the only-begotten Son of God."[62] Calvin may at times speak as though God in some unknowable way descended in order that he might appear to men,[63] but he has statements which guard these from misunderstanding: "Whenever he manifested himself to the fathers, Christ was the Mediator between him and them; who not only personates God in proclaiming his word, but is also truly and essentially God."[64] It may have been that Calvin considered God himself as out of relation with men, whereas Christ and the Holy Spirit shared the being-in-relation office. The point, however, is that Calvin did "demythologize" the language about God in the Bible and in so doing found it necessary to explain away the natural meaning of the language.

Moderation and the Christian Life

To Calvin the ideal of the Christian life was moderation. He derived this ideal from his understanding of the life, ministry, and teaching of Jesus Christ. There could scarcely be a more important admonition to men in relation to the pursuit of their vocation than to follow the example of Christ in this respect. Calvin finds this ideal exemplified in Jesus' retirement in Galilee, explaining that it was not so much that Jesus was unwilling to be known but rather that he desired "to pursue his course with regularity, and in such a manner as he judged to be proper."[65] Every man has a good deal to learn from this: "Hence too we hear that our minds ought to be regulated in such a manner that, on the one hand, we may not be deterred by any fear from going forward in duty; and that, on the other hand, we may not too rashly throw ourselves into dangers. All who are earnestly desirous to pursue their calling will be careful to maintain this moderation."[66]

This ideal of moderation was behind Calvin's aversion to the excess of human feelings, which was in sharp contrast to the tenor of life in the late Middle Ages, which Huizinga described, with reserve, as a "general facility of emotions, of tears and spiritual upheavals."[67] Jesus Christ again set the example which Calvin urged upon his readers. Calvin may occasionally note that Jesus was momentarily overtaken by a vehemence of desire, but he adds that Christ, unlike us, never withdrew "his mind from pure moderation (*puram moderationem*)."[68] Certainly Jesus took upon himself the same weakness of the flesh with which we are saddled, but there is a real difference. "In us there is no affection unaccompanied by sin, because they all exceed due bounds and proper restraint; but when Christ was distressed by grief and fear, he did not rise against God, but continued to be regulated by the true rule of moderation."[69]

It is interesting that Calvin's point was not that human feelings in themselves are bad, but rather that they are in fact bad because we are not able to control them.[70] Calvin considered that before the fall all of men's feelings were subject to reason and that this was the case with Christ.[71] It is almost as though Calvin favored a golden mean. He certainly did not think our religion condemns all personal care or concern. It condemns only the excess of concern "which proceeds from an immoderate and blind attachment to ourselves."[72] The passage in the Sermon on the Mount in which we are forbidden to be anxious Calvin understands to be a prohibition of "excessive" anxiety. "We know that men are born on the condition of having some care; and, indeed, this is not the least portion of the miseries, which the Lord has laid upon us as a punishment, in order to humble us. But immoderate care is condemned."[73]

This rule of moderation is carried over into Calvin's interpretation of the Christian ethic. Apparently without exception Calvin employs his exegetical ingenuity to moderate the most rigorous demands of the gospel ethic. In a day when the rigor of Jesus' ethic has again been brought to light,[74] this emphasis by Calvin can hardly escape notice. It is particularly striking in his interpretation of the Sermon on the Mount. In the early part of that discourse where Jesus reinterprets the law saying, "You have heard that it was said . . . but I say to you . . . ," Calvin sees Jesus as neither abrogating nor extending the law but rather as giving the law its true interpretation. For the most part this consists in making explicit the spiritual interpretation which Moses actually intended. But in the case of Jesus' injunction against swearing, Calvin is forced to interpret in such a way that Jesus is made to mean something quite different from what he actually says. This prohibition means that one should not swear lightly rather than that he should not swear at all.[75] In this Calvin is dependent on two premises in addition to his proclivity to moderation: (1) The law does not condemn oaths, and (2) Jesus did not alter the law. "It hence appears that it was not Christ's design . . . to abolish oaths altogether, but on the contrary to call attention to the due observance of the law; and the law, allowing an oath, only condemns perjury and needless swearing."[76]

With other radical demands Calvin is equally moderating, and the Mosaic Law is not always a contributing factor. A statement such as "If your right eye causes you to sin, pluck it out" (Matt. 5:29) is dismissed as "an exaggerated form of speech."[77] As for Jesus' correction of the eye-for-eye and tooth-for-tooth ethic, Calvin understands it simply as a prohibition of private revenge.[78] Turning the other cheek cannot be taken as a rule of life because it would be an encouragement to wrongdoers, and the injunction to give the cloak when someone takes the coat is foolish: "None but a fool will stand upon the words, so as to maintain, that we must yield to our opponents what they demand, before coming into a court of law."[79] The injunction only means that the Christian should be prepared to lose everything if the case goes against him.[80] Jesus never intended that we should give to *anyone* who asks. He only meant to make his disciples generous. "It would be a foolish prodigality to scatter at random what the Lord has given us."[81] The disciples are taught "not to think that they have discharged their duty when they have aided a few persons, but to study to be kind to all, and not to be weary of giving, so long as they have the means."[82] To say the least, this modifies considerably the rigorous quality of Jesus' statement. In the same way Calvin decides that the intention of Jesus in commanding the young man to sell everything and give it to the poor was to teach men self-denial.[83] John's command to his disciples that none of them should have two coats is understood as a use of synecdoche of which the lesson is that "each person should give out of his abundance to supply the wants of the poor."[84]

One of the most difficult statements in the gospels is reported in Luke 14:26: "If any one comes to me and does not hate his own father and mother and wife and children and brothers and sisters, yes, and even his own life, he cannot be my disciple." So far as Calvin can see, the meaning of this is no different from the meaning of the parallel statement in Matthew 10:37: "He who loves father or mother more than me is not worthy of me." Although in other instances of divergent parallels Calvin was prone to take the most inclusive statement or the one which could embody the other in its own natural meaning, that is not the case here at all. Calvin covers both texts with a paraphrase which moderates even the milder statement in Matthew: "If the love of ourselves hinder us from following Christ, we must resist it courageously."[85]

Calvin also moderates the prohibition of judging. "These words of Christ do not contain an absolute prohibition from judging, but are intended to cure a disease, which appears to be natural to us all."[86] The interpretation of the story in John of the woman taken in adultery is an interesting application of Calvin's view on judging. It will be recalled that the scribes and Pharisees brought this woman to Jesus to see what punishment, if any, Jesus would recommend, knowing that the law demanded that adulterers be stoned. Although Calvin criticizes the scribes and Pharisees for not being witnesses and judges against themselves, he sides with them on the other point. The woman should have been stoned. "Indeed, there will be no crime whatever that shall not be exempted from the penalties of the law, if adultery be not punished."[87] Calvin claims that punishment was not Christ's office, but then adds, "While Christ forgives the sins of men, he does not overturn political order, or reverse the sentences and punishments."[88] In this way Calvin takes this story as an opportunity to emphasize the necessity of judging![89]

The same twist of interpretation prevails in Calvin's comments on the parable of the wheat and the tares. The point of the parable is that one can do nothing about the weeds growing along with the wheat until the harvest. Calvin will not allow this to be taken in such a way as to prevent judgment or the purification of the Church now. In his exegesis he opens the way by determining what is meant by the wheat and the tares. It cannot be doctrine; Christ would never have forbidden this kind of purging. He finally decides that the parable must refer to those faults in morals which cannot be corrected, "but we are not at liberty to extend such a toleration to wicked errors, which corrupt the purity of faith."⁹⁰

Again, Calvin's views on judging are governed by the rule of moderation: "It is not necessary that believers should become blind, and perceive nothing, but only that they should refrain from an *undue* eagerness to judge: for otherwise the *proper bounds* of rigour will be exceeded by every man who desires to pass sentence on his brethren."⁹¹ The ideal of moderation as a principle of interpretation was dictated to Calvin partly by his determination to maintain the unity of scripture and partly by his own fondness for the golden mean. In either case a departure from the natural meaning of texts was required.

Related partly to his ideal of moderation and partly to his conviction of the unerring character of those who wrote scripture is Calvin's unusual interpretation of the prophets. In the present day prophets are often seen as figures who underwent intense struggles between their compassion for the people and their visions of the impending and irrevocable judgment of God. They were ecstatic figures, but their zeal for the righteousnes of their God was often realized at the cost of deep strife with their own personal reluctance to proclaim the unmistakable message. Calvin's view was quite different from this. His understanding of the prophets was succinctly stated in his comment on Ezekiel 3:14: "God's prophets were of a sedate and composed mind."⁹²

The application of the conception of the prophetic character is most striking in the exegesis of what contemporary critics call Jeremiah's confessions. These are sections in the book of that prophet in which Jeremiah describes in the most intense way his own hatred of the work to which he has been called and the overwhelming power of God in his body and spirit. On the one hand, he contends severely with God and curses the day of his birth, while, on the other hand, he confesses that the word of God was to him like a fire and that it was felt even in the marrow of his bones. This can hardly be construed as an example of moderation.

To Calvin, however, this is precisely what it was. At one point, where Jeremiah has disputed with God about the triumph of the wicked and is rebuked by God for it, Calvin comments, "Many think that God here checks the boldness of Jeremiah, as though he had exceeded the limits of moderation when he contended with God."[93] This supposition, however, is quickly denied. Calvin claims that the prophet was not presumptuous, but rather, speaking "through a divine fervour" and "influenced by God," he sought to "rouse an obstinate people."[94]

In the well-known place where Jeremiah bemoans his birth because of the burden he has been made to bear (Jer. 15:10), Calvin admits that the prophet displayed his weakness, but not really. "It must however be observed, that he was so restrained by the secret power of the Holy Spirit, that he did not break forth intemperately."[95] He always kept the aim of the public good in mind. True, the passage shows that he was not so calm and composed as to ward off anger when his words accomplished less than he desired, "and yet it is evident from the context, that all this was expressed for the benefit of the public."[96] It looks like an expression of intemperate feeling when Jeremiah implicates his mother in his misery. It even seems that he attributes part of the blame to her because she bore him. "Now this appears unreasonable. But it may at the same time be easily gathered, that the Prophet was not led away by so great a vehemence, except for the sake of promoting the public good, and that it was for this end that he uttered his complaint."[97] What he really means to say by this is that his readers should ask his mother if he has always been contentious. Calvin paraphrases: "Has my mother been the cause why ye say that I am a turbulent man and the author of strifes? Doubtless nothing can be imputed to my mother; and I am as innocent as she is."[98]

Some explanation for Jeremiah's struggle is always available. In one place the struggle is calculated by the prophet in order that men would not think him hardhearted.[99] Where Jeremiah claims that God has deceived him, Calvin claims that the language is ironical.[100] In another place, where the prophet curses outright the day of his birth, the exegete decides that the whole passage refers to an earlier history which Jeremiah relates in order to show the greatness of God's mercy in having delivered him. Only because this struggle took place before the prophetic call can Calvin judge it inexcusable and assert that Jeremiah was "led away as it were by an insane impulse."[101]

Summary

Calvin operated with a conception of scripture as authoritative and errorless. This does not mean that everything which is condoned in the scripture can be a pattern for our lives. There are exceptions. We should not follow the example of Moses in killing the Egyptian,[102] and Jeremiah was a little hasty in imprecating final destruction on his enemies;[103] but these exceptions, as well as others, were prompted by the Holy Spirit. Indeed, Calvin thought that Moses was not as bold as he should have been in murdering the Egyptian.

Despite these few exceptions, however, the fact that Calvin took the Bible as a whole as setting the pattern for our lives made it possible for him to fasten on the vengeance Psalms and assume on biblical grounds an attitude that can only be reminiscent of the prayer of the Pharisee in the parable. It is quite strange that Calvin, who repeatedly emphasized the necessity of putting one's glory in God and debasing oneself, could combine this attitude with a forceful self-justification. "David, therefore, in order to pray aright, reposes himself in the word and promise of God; and the import of his exercise is this: Lord, I am not led by ambition, or foolish headstrong passion, or depraved desire, inconsiderately to ask from thee whatever is pleasing to my flesh; but it is the clear light of thy word which directs me, and upon it I securely depend."[104] Evidently once one takes refuge in the word and promise of God, those feelings are justified which are comparable to the feelings that prevented the Pharisee from being justified. In commenting on another Psalm he asserts that this is one purpose in living righteously. "By this form of prayer the Holy Spirit teaches us, that we ought diligently to endeavour to live an upright and innocent life, so that, if there are any who give us trouble, we may be able to boast that we are blamed and persecuted wrongfully."[105]

The problem is that there is no key for determining what is an exception and what is not, for knowing what is to be taken in one way and what in another. Evidently a good deal is dependent on the exegete, but we have seen that a number of problems are associated with determining the work of the Spirit in the interpreter.

For himself Calvin saw no problem at all in interpretation. Everything about it was obvious and simple to him. His exegesis is repeatedly saturated with phrases which emphasize the simplicity of the task at hand and the unmistakable character of the conclusion. The most frequent expressions are: *certum est* or *certe* (it is certain, unquestionably),[106] *responsio facilis est, facilis est solutio, solutio in promptu est* or *facilis est conciliatio* (the answer, solution or reconciliation is easy),[107] *scimus* (we know),[108] and *dubium non est* (there is no doubt).[109] Always the exegete's mind was incredibly clear.

When we set this facility of interpretation alongside the moderation of the rigor in the Sermon on the Mount, we may see that although Calvin was sternly moral he had an oversimplified ethic, and although he was rigidly biblical he had an overconfidence in interpretation. This certainty in exegesis was based on the certainty of the divine source of scripture. Any exegesis that supported this conviction was right. Calvin, with his mastery of the Bible and his ingenuity of mind, found this easy. The irony of his situation, however, is apparent when he must overlook or deny the natural meaning of the inspired text in order to uphold its unity.

Before turning to another topic I should like to state once more that the purpose of this chapter has not been to give a full and balanced picture of Calvin as an interpreter of the Bible. That would have been extrinsic to the subject of this essay. On the contrary, I have focused particularly on those exegetical tools and patterns which point to difficulties in the theory of the unity of the Bible as Calvin understood it. To concentrate in this way on the defects in an exegetical career which overall is remarkably impressive certainly does not prove that the Bible is not a unity. It does, however, indicate that Calvin himself had to take recourse on occasion to rather devious techniques and notions in order to maintain his theory, and it suggests something of the gargantuan task facing anyone who holds that the Bible from beginning to end is internally consistent.

The Response of the Believer
to the Knowledge

Calvin was so thoroughly convinced of the divine causality as well as of the denial of free will in men that a consistent determinism might be expected from him. In a certain sense Calvin was consistently deterministic. He held that nothing has ever happened and that nothing will ever happen without the express direction of God. However, this did not mean for Calvin that one could overlook or minimize human responsibility. The Bible commands us to exhort; so we exhort, and we should expect men to respond to our exhortation. Nor did it mean that he had no regard for human feelings, or that he paid no attention to the human reactions consequent to given acts, events, or circumstances.

Because of this Calvin had a good deal to say about the response of the believer to the knowledge available to him in the Christian faith. As we look into the nature of this response we complete the battery of questions we posed to the problem of knowledge in Chapter III.

Certainty

The most striking impression which comes with reading the work of Calvin is the unfailing certainty which pervades the whole corpus. In Chapter I we observed that Calvin was a man obsessed by the desire for certainty, and we saw how carefully he worked out a principle of authority in the correlation of word and Spirit which, because of the all-pervasiveness of the divine activity in it, would be productive of that certainty. By subordinating all uncertain authorities he put himself under the control of this certain one. Having investigated the work of the Spirit, which makes certain the word, and having examined the character and content of the knowledge derived from the certain word, we shall now look into the nature of this certainty itself since it is one aspect of the believer's response to Christian knowledge.

As might be expected, there is a discernible distinction in the nature of certainty comparable to the distinction already noted in the character of knowledge. When Calvin writes of the certainty associated with faith it is an intensely personal thing which he has in mind. It is the certainty of one's own future adoption that is sealed by the testimony of the Holy Spirit.[1] In Calvin's mind the notion of certainty fits quite properly with the term "persuasion," which is central in his discussion of faith. A person is "firmly persuaded"[2] or "certainly persuaded"[3] that Christ is his and that God's free grace is his through Christ. This certainty that is the consequence of faith may even be used as a more appropriate description of the knowledge of faith than the more cognitive term "comprehension." "The knowledge of faith consists more in certainty than in comprehension."[4]

This most crucial of all matters is certain because, although it is only held in the most personal and inward way, it is assured by that which is outside us. Men are always weak and much too prone to waver. If left to themselves salvation would be utterly inconceivable. "Our salvation is certain, because it is in the hand of God."[5] One finds one's repose in God, in whom there is the only possible surety, and this assurance is true by virtue of a deeply spiritual conviction and experience. It is interesting that this kind of certainty leads directly to self-abasement and humility. The Roman Catholics, Calvin writes, "complain that this certainty of confidence is chargeable with arrogance and presumption. But as we ought to presume nothing of ourselves, so we should presume everything of God."[6]

On the other hand, the certainty associated with the wider knowledge, like the character of that knowledge, is rather objective and external to the knower. This certainty is created "by oracles, by the law, and by the prophets."[7] It is in the authority of these oracles that one can have confidence, and only by speaking with them can one rid one's discourse of uncertainty.[8] As a matter of fact, the very purpose of a precisely correct scripture is "to prevent us from wavering in perpetual uncertainty."[9] This kind of certainty is more nearly related to the cognitive functions. Since "the Scripture is the school of the Holy Spirit, in which, as nothing necessary and useful to be known is omitted," and "nothing is taught which it is not beneficial to know, . . . we must recur to the word of the Lord, which affords a certain rule for the understanding."[10] In short, this is an objective certainty derived from the objective word, and in this vein Calvin speaks quite easily of "certain" conclusions.[11]

A further distinction might be drawn on the basis of the order involved between knowledge and certainty. Faith is called knowledge by Calvin because it is certain; the whole scope of instruction is certain because it is derived from the book of knowledge. Just above we pointed out that Calvin thought certainty was a more apt description of faith than comprehension. It is this character of certainty in faith that justifies its being called knowledge. "Let this truth then stand sure,—that no one can be called a son of God, who does not know himself to be such; and this is called knowledge by John, in order to set forth its certainty (I John 5:19, 20)."[12] Quite different, it seems, is the wider knowledge. In the chapter on providence, when Calvin begins to refute a theory of natural causation by listing the reasons against it, he cuts himself short. He decides this way is much too tedious and that it should be sufficient to rest content with the authority of God himself. Then he calls attention to the special providence of God related in the Bible and concludes, "If we believe these things it is certain that not a drop of rain falls but at the express command of God."[13] In contrast to the former reference we have here a bit of information that is certain because it is derived from the book of knowledge.

A distinction in the character of certainty may also be found in Calvin's attitude toward doubt. There is no place at all for doubt about the absolute authority of the Bible in its totality. If there is to be any right knowledge of God at all it will come from the Bible, and if one has a doubt about any part of the scripture it means that one's knowledge will be uncertain. This is why Calvin finds it necessary to introduce the discussion of the work of the Spirit in confirming the belief in the scripture so early in Book I. At this point he thinks he must "remove every doubt" about the authority of the Bible.[14] The activity of the Holy Spirit is the only conceivable way of removing such doubt. Until men are illuminated by his testimony, "they are perpetually fluctuating amidst a multitude of doubts."[15] After that, however, there is "an entire acquiescence in the Scripture."[16]

That Calvin was adamant in this conviction may be seen from his conflicts in the city of Geneva. When Sebastian Castellio, who came to Geneva in 1542 as rector of the school, applied for admission to the pastorate in order to have an adequate income for his large family, Calvin vigorously opposed the application and led the Genevan pastors in rejecting it. Calvin's quarrel with Castellio had to do with the latter's divergence on a few points of doctrine and the language he used in translating the Bible, but the main point of dispute was Castellio's criticism of the Song of Solomon. Castellio felt the book was an obscene description of the author's love affairs. Calvin, like almost everyone else in his day, interpreted the book quite freely as descriptive of the relation between Christ and his church. To consider the book debased threatened his entire structure of biblical authority. On the canon as on any part of the scripture there can be no doubt concerning authorship.[17]

Calvin reacted in the same way when in 1551 and 1552 his understanding of the doctrine of double predestination was challenged first by Jerome Hermes Bolsec and then by Jean Trolliet. Probably in both cases Calvin's animosity was stirred by the implication that he himself was not adequate as an interpreter of scripture, but it is safe to say that his uncompromising stand was prompted more by the threat to the word as a whole, which he supposed this doubt to create. The word of God is certain, and double predestination is certainly declared therein. One cannot doubt the one without doubting the other, and that cannot be allowed. In both cases Calvin fought with all his strength until he was supported by the Little Council.[18]

There is, then, no provision whatsoever for doubt about the truth of the full contents of scripture, and with regard to the certainty of faith it would be wrong to suggest that Calvin freely allowed for doubt. Nonetheless the character of faith's certainty did allow for an element of doubt. "Some portion of unbelief," he stated, "is always mixed with faith in every Christian."[19] This mixture is clearly explained when he describes the certainty of faith. "When we inculcate that faith ought to be certain and secure, we conceive not of a certainty attended with no doubt, or of a security interrupted by no anxiety; but we rather affirm, that believers have a perpetual conflict with their own diffidence, and are far from placing their consciences in a placid calm, never disturbed by any storms."[20] In must be understood, however, that this element of doubt does not endanger the doctrine of perseverance in the faith. If one has really been elected by God this doubt will not be fatal. "We deny, however they may be afflicted, that they ever fall and depart from that certain confidence which they have conceived in the Divine mercy."[21]

The reason for such doubt is clear, and it points back to the intensely personal character of the knowledge of faith. Something as inward as this is bound to be affected—slightly at least—by the person. The person, of course, is weak and sinful, and this will create some fluctuation and doubt. "The pious heart therefore perceives a division in itself, being partly affected with delight, through a knowledge of the Divine goodness; partly distressed with sorrow, through a sense of its own calamity; partly relying on the promise of the gospel; partly trembling at the evidence of its own iniquity; partly exulting in the apprehension of life; partly alarmed by the fear of death."[22] This statement, too, must be read with caution lest it be misunderstood. Calvin does not mean that faith is therefore uncertain or unclear and that it is "an obscure and perplexed knowledge of the Divine will respecting us."[23] To be distracted does not mean to be divested of faith; to be harassed does not mean to be cast into the abyss; to be shaken does not mean to be overthrown.[24]

Even this much doubt, if it found its way into one's attitude toward the Bible as a whole, would wreck the whole structure of authority. In the case of faith, however, it is possible to conceive of a doubt-in-certainty in which both the doubt and the certainty are quite real and true. Only one must be careful not to make too much of this. Even while allowing for doubt in faith, Calvin could argue with characteristic vigor against the "diabolical opinion" of the Papists "that we ought to doubt our final perseverance, because we are uncertain whether we shall be to-morrow in the same state of grace. . . . How weak soever we may then be," he asserts, "yet our salvation is not uncertain, because it is sustained by God's power. Hence is its security, not only for the present, but also for the future."[25] There is nothing quite so severe then as Luther's *anfechtungen,* his terrible depressions or bouts with the devil, and certainly nothing so extreme as the ultimate doubt so often characteristic in the present day, but there is harassment, distraction, a degree of shaking—all against a background of certainty.

Trust and Obedience

Some have supposed that Calvin's strong emphasis on knowledge in his interpretation of the Christian faith denotes an overemphasis on the intellectual. Dowey has called attention to Albrecht Ritschl's unfavorable criticism of Calvin on this point as against Martin Luther, who understood faith as trust.[26] However, the two Reformers were perhaps no more divergent in their views on the understanding of faith than they were on any other point.

Calvin's understanding of faith as knowledge is certainly no more an intellectual approach than the writings of John in the New Testament. We have already seen the intensely personal character of this knowledge. Although Calvin consistently spoke of faith as *cognitio,* it was not cognition in the way that term is most generally understood. The word was applicable to faith more because of its personal certainty than because of any comprehension of the mind. In the same way, and closely related to that notion of certainty, the most natural response of the believer to the gift of faith was understood to be *fiducia*—trust or confidence. These two meanings of the word are related. Trust emphasizes the trustworthiness of the object of one's faith; confidence points to the boldness of the one who believes.

Calvin's definition of faith has within it the doctrine of election. Faith is a gift; it comes by the activity of the Holy Spirit, not by anything a man can do. When Calvin discusses the doctrine of election more fully, he states that one of the main functions of this doctrine, which is first discussed after the doctrine of faith, is to give one a "solid confidence" (*solidae fiduciae*—a certain trust).[27] This is one of the most proper responses to faith. The one who believes is the one who prays. But what does one pray—or rather, what can one pray? Of and by himself a man could pray nothing at all. Once he has received the gift of faith and responds with trust, however, he can pray boldly. Only the "elect possess that confidence (*fiduciam*—trust), which Paul celebrates, so as boldly to 'cry, Abba, Father' (Gal. 4:6)."[28] Faith and trust are, as it were, inseparable; the one will always follow the other. "To separate faith from trust (*fiducia*) would be equal to an attempt to separate heat and light from the sun."[29]

Entirely consistent with this understanding of *fiducia* as the response to faith are other descriptions of the response, such as new life. "When God illuminates us with the knowledge of himself, he is said to raise us from death, and to make us new creatures (John 5:25)."[30] This new life is an experience in the present to him to whom the Spirit has witnessed the reality of God's gratuitous goodness. "Whoever confines his whole attention to the earthly nature of the flesh, will find in it nothing but what is dead; but they who shall raise their eyes to the power of the Spirit, which is diffused over the flesh, will learn from the actual effect and from the experience of faith, that it is not without reason that it is called quickening."[31]

When we introduce terms like "quickening" and "new life" as the response of faith, as well as when we compare faith and trust by analogy with the sun and its light and heat, it is questionable if the term "response" is appropriate for the discussion. Quickening, new life, and trust are not things that a man does. Calvin did not use them as the object of exhortation. These are what one may expect from faith. In this sense they are not responses. They are effects—the inevitable outcome of true faith. Whether one speaks of them as responses or effects, however, they are the most appropriate descriptions of what follows from the knowledge of faith.

The most frequently mentioned response to knowledge where

the biblical material is the source—and also the most appropriate corollary to authority as that word is most often understood—is obedience. Calvin was a prophet of obedience, and one may even consider this statement, which appears early in the *Institutes,* as one of the dominant mottoes of his life: "For obedience is the source, not only of an absolutely perfect and complete faith, but of all right knowledge of God."[32] That this statement appears in the chapter on the work of the Holy Spirit in confirming the scriptures is instructive. By far the most common occurence of the plea for obedience is in relation to the more heteronomous authority —in short, in relation to the Bible as a whole. In the tenth chapter of Book IV, where Calvin combats the Papists for having arrogated to themselves the power of making legislation, he proclaims God as the "sole legislator," giving two reasons:

> The first is, that his will may be received as the perfect rule of all righteousness and holiness, and so that an acquaintance with it may be all the knowledge necessary to a good life. The second is, that with respect to the mode of worshipping him aright, he may exercise the sole empire over our souls, to whom we are under the strongest obligation to obey his authority and await his commands (*cui parere et a cuius nutu pendere debeamus*).[33]

Since the ruin of the human race came about because Adam and Eve departed from a command of God, it is for the keeping of the commands of God that the elect must exercise utmost care. There is only one source in which these commands may be surely known—the Bible. Thus it is necessary for men to obey his word (*obedimus eius verbo*) if there is to be any security in worship.[34] Calvin's argument often sounds like an exercise in deductive logic. Obedience is necessary in the elect. The obedience to God depends on the knowledge of God's will. The will of God is certainly known only in the law. The elect must obey the law of God revealed in the scripture. "God hath revealed unto us his will in the law (*in lege*); wherefore, those men do obey (*obediunt*) God, who do that alone which is agreeable to the law of God; and, again, which submit (*subiiciunt*) themselves willingly to his government (*eius imperio*)."[35]

This obedience is perhaps the cardinal virtue in men. It is

inconceivable to Calvin that a man could love God without "submitting (*submittat*) entirely to his authority."[36] It appears that the highest obedience is that which submits without question or even without understanding. Calvin's comments on the washing of the disciples' feet in John 13 seem to indicate this. It will be remembered that Peter objected when Jesus began to wash his feet. Jesus told Peter he would understand this act later, but Peter persisted in his refusal. When Jesus explained, "If I do not wash you, you have no part in me," Peter submitted and asked that Jesus wash not only his feet but his hands and head as well. Calvin comments that Peter's modesty might have been commendable "were it not that obedience is of greater value in the sight of God than any nod of honour or service." He continues by explaining that "the true and only rule of humility" is

> to yield ourselves in obedience to God (*subiicere nos in obsequium Dei*), and to have all our senses regulated by his good pleasure, so that every thing which he declares to be agreeable to Him shall also be approved by us, without any scruple. We ought, therefore, above all, to observe this rule of serving God, that we shall be always ready to acquiesce (*subscribere*), without delay, as soon as he issues any command (*aliquid mandat*).[37]

It is not necessary for one to understand why one should do a particular thing. The only thing of importance is to know that it is a command of God, and this knowledge is available in the scriptures.

If obedience is the active response corresponding to the commands of God revealed in the Bible, then the passive response corresponding to the teaching of God in scripture is docility. Obedience was strongly emphasized as the reverse of that which brought on the ruin of man in the first place. This ruin, of course, affected human understanding, with the result that men will never gain wisdom from themselves. It will only come "by submissively receiving what God teaches us both by his Word and by his Holy Spirit."[38] The dominant place Calvin gave to this submission is in a way surprising. Calvin fought vigorously against the Roman Catholic doctrine of implicit faith. The idea that a believer could rest content by simply believing whatever the Church should teach, even if he did not know the Church's teaching, was in Calvin's mind the most gross aberration. As it turns out, however, Calvin himself upholds a form of implicit faith which differs from the Catholic variety only in its object. If the Roman Church holds that the believer must submit implicitly to the teaching of the Church, Calvin holds the same thing with regard to the Bible. "It must be remembered," he writes, "that every word which may have issued forth from God is to be received with implicit authority."[39] This difference in the object of belief was an important one for Calvin. The Church is made up of men, and it is subject to human errors; but the Bible is ours through the work of the Holy Spirit. Moreover, Calvin did insist strongly that the believer should move steadily toward a more complete knowledge by the continued study of his authority.

The important thing is that the believer's response to this authority in his study should be docility. The Psalmist shows us "what kind of scholars God requires, namely, those who are fools in their own estimation (I Cor. 3:18), and who come down to the rank of children, that the loftiness of their own understanding may not prevent them from giving themselves up, with a spirit of entire docility (*dociles*), to the teaching of the word of God (*Dei verbo*)."[40] In Calvin's main autobiographical comment we learn that the production of docility was the key result of his conversion.

> And first, since I was too obstinately devoted to the superstitions of Popery to be easily extricated from so profound an abyss of mire, God by a sudden conversion (*par une conversion subite / subita conversionem*) subdued and brought my mind to a teachable frame (to docility: *à docilité / ad docilitatem*) which was more hardened in such matters than might have been expected from one at my early period of life.[41]

In the discussion of obedience we saw that understanding cannot be construed as a prerequisite for doing the commands of God. The bare declaration of a command in the Bible should be sufficient to prompt the believer into action even though it may seem contrary to his understanding of things. That is also the case with docility. There are many things that the human mind cannot comprehend. This does not mean, however, that one's range of knowledge must be severely limited. Comprehension is not necessary to knowledge. Two things only are necessary: an authoritative source and a docile mind. True wisdom will not be extracted from reason or gained through education. "Our wisdom ought to consist in embracing with gentle docility (*mansueta docilitate*), and without exception (*sine exceptione*), all that is delivered in the sacred Scriptures."[42]

It can readily be seen that Calvin's stress on docility corresponds to his stress on the rather objective teaching of scripture and to his insistence on the authority of scripture in its totality. Docility along with obedience is the counterpart to an authority of this nature. "There must be docility, in order that God's word may obtain credit, authority, and favour among us."[43] It also corresponds, therefore, to Calvin's positivistic use of the scriptures for proofs of one kind or another. In one place Calvin rebukes the disclaimers of original sin in this way: "Since, however, none but God alone is a proper judge in this cause, we must acquiesce (*acquiescendum est*) in the sentence which he has pronounced in the Scriptures. In the first place, Scripture clearly teaches us that we are born vicious and perverse."[44] It may be added that docility also corresponds in the same way with the discussion of the necessity of interpreters and the high place given in Calvin's theology to the pastors of the Church. It is God's will that all believers should be reared under the education of the Church. For this purpose he has raised up leaders and has given them the office of preaching the heavenly doctrine. "We see that all are placed under the same regulation, in order that they may submit themselves with gentleness and docility of mind (*mansueto et docili spiritu*) to be governed by the pastors who are appointed for this purpose."[45]

This docility and obedience are produced by the work of the Holy Spirit. It is his office "to bend our hearts to obedience."[46] This is the significance of God's writing the law on our hearts. As long as the law is written only on stone tablets there is no chance of our being affected by it because of our depraved condition. We are able to embrace the commands of God obediently only "when by his Spirit he changes and corrects the natural depravity of our hearts."[47] It is because men are utterly incapable of governing themselves, then, that they must give themselves up to be governed by God, and this depends on the Spirit working in our hearts to create a confidence in the scriptures as a whole and to produce obedience to the will of God declared in them.[48]

Because Calvin believed that the man of faith would have no confidence in himself and supreme confidence in Holy Scripture, he could look upon obedience and docility not so much as human responses to Christian knowledge but rather as effects. The gospel, he declares, "produces of itself reverence, fear, and obedience."[49] In order to guard himself against the criticism that his emphasis on obedience means that men have a necessary share in their salvation, he makes it quite clear that obedience "is not the cause why he [Christ] continues his love toward us, but is rather the effect of his love."[50] Obedience and docility, then, are effects just as trust and new life are effects. The difference is only in the components of the equation: If a person believes that God is gratuitously merciful toward him, he will trust in God and have the experience of new life; if he believes that the scriptures have come to us through the dictation of the Holy Spirit, he will submit himself with docility to the teaching of the Bible and will diligently obey the commands of God contained in it.

It has been repeatedly stated that Calvin himself made very little out of the distinction we have been pursuing. He pays no attention to the implications of the use of two distinctly different vocabularies—one with reference to the full knowledge of the Bible, the other with reference to faith in the divine promises. It is no problem to him because the knowledge of God's benevolence toward us is contained in the unquestioned wider knowledge of the Bible as a whole. Furthermore, he assumed that a conviction about the Bible as a whole is a corollary of faith in the divine mercy. If we submit to God's word of promise, Calvin reasoned, we will also submit to whatever God has said, and Calvin, like Luther and like other medieval Christians, never doubted that the Bible was God's speech. Calvin's own statement of the distinction, as we observed in Chapter III, does not go beyond what he said in the chapter on faith in the *Institutes*.

That fact should again be emphasized here. For Calvin obedience could in no way be distinguished from faith. In his mind obedience is below, in, and beyond faith. On the one hand, he could write, "The basis of true religion is obedience."[51] On the other hand, he could state, "Faith is properly that by which we obey the gospel,"[52] and he could speak freely of "the obedience of faith."[53] Beyond this, as we have seen, he was certain that obedience will always follow faith. Indeed, one can be sure that if a man does not obey God he does not know him as Lord and Father, as he shews himself, without being dutiful children and obedient servants."[54]

Obedience pervaded the whole of Calvin's theology, and it is always associated with the commands of God and thus with a legalistic understanding of the Christian faith. Actually, Calvin saw no distinction at all in the content of the Law and the Gospel. He made this clear in his discussions of the differences and similarities between the Old and New Testaments. In these discussions the weight falls in the direction of the gratuitous promises. Calvin tried to show that the Old Testament fathers as well as the men and women of the New Testament placed their hope in the mercy of God revealed in Christ. The main difference was that the revelation is shadowy in the Old Testament whereas it is bright and clear in the New. This tendency to identify the two testaments could, however, be turned around. The Gospel is no less law than the Law itself. The only difference between them has to do with power rather than with content. "He now shews a difference between the Law and the Gospel, for the Gospel brings with it the grace of regeneration: its doctrine, therefore, is not that of the letter, but penetrates into the heart and reforms all the inward faculties, so that obedience is rendered to the righteousness of God."[55]

When we couple this with Calvin's account of his own conversion, in which the dominant motif is the creation by God of a teachable frame, we can only conclude that obedience along with the view of the scriptures and the conception of authority which it entails was the foundation rock on which Calvin's structure of theology was built. Despite this fact, however, it must also be clear that his understanding of faith as a knowledge of God's gratuitous mercy toward us, along with the somewhat different conception of authority implied by that, was the vital nerve of his theology. Both of these were derived from a correlation of the word and the Spirit. Although the way in which the word was understood was not necessarily the same for both of them, and although the character of the knowledge and the nature of the Spirit's work is distinguishable in each instance, nevertheless Calvin could not have conceived a critical separation.

It is significant for the contemporary understanding of Calvin that such a critical separation is consistently possible on the basis of an analysis of his own language, but it is also important to observe that for this sixteenth-century figure a distinction of this sort was not only unthinkable but unnecessary. The vibrant, personal faith which constitutes the core of his *Institutes* was legitimately derived from his more rigid and objective point of departure. Whether that particular foundation is necessary or even appropriate to the core is another question.

END OF PART III

Epilogue

Calvin, Later Calvinism, and the Contemporary Situation

That other question must be asked: What is the necessary and appropriate foundation for the conception of authority in the Christian faith? When that question is posed, others follow. What are the source, the character, and the content of knowledge available to the Christian? What is the nature of its certainty? This essay has sought to analyze the thought of one historical figure on the question governed by the conviction that the study of one to whom the authority of the Bible was central would prove to be enlightening in the contemporary situation where the Bible has once again become central and the problem of authority crucial.

As we have seen, Calvin's principle of authority in the correlation of word and Spirit stood for a number of things in which a significant duality is discernible. One can readily understand why Calvin drew no thoroughgoing distinction between the two species of knowledge derived from his one conception of authority. It is because he basically conceived authority in terms of the Bible as an objective book of knowledge which one is to accept with an attitude of docility. Nonetheless he realized that docility and credulity are insufficient as long as their object remains unrelated. A meaning of real significance occurs only as the unrelated becomes *erga me*. This, Calvin thought, can only take place through the internal testimony of the Holy Spirit. With the introduction of this element his theology took on its dual cast.

Both aspects are derived from the same principle of authority, the interrelationship of the scriptures and the work of the Holy Spirit. In actuality, however, one can use the one word "authority" in speaking of faith and the wider knowledge only because of the ambiguity inherent in the term. The wider knowledge is authoritative in a way analogous to that in which the law of the land is authoritative to a law-abiding citizen. It is external to the person and stands over against him. The knowledge of faith is authoritative because it reacts upon the person persuasively and becomes the basis on which the life of that person is reordered.

So there are actually two conceptions. The dynamic is derived from the static, but the dynamic also reacts upon the static. Calvin went far in making some of the most difficult doctrines come alive. In his exposition of the divine providence his usually studied prose becomes quite unself-conscious and ecstatic. The conviction that one's life is in the hands of God, come what may, is, without doubt, a force of liberation. Something similar may be said about Calvin's teaching on predestination and even the angels. There is often a strong dynamic in the theology, but it is only where doctrines are related to the doctrine of faith. Where he describes the objective matter-of-fact situation, the most appropriate terms for the acceptance of what he says are, again, docility and obedience, and this remains lifeless even when buttressed by a claim for the internal testimony of the Holy Spirit.

Insofar as Calvin gave expression to the dynamic quality of the Christian faith he echoed in his own way Luther's rediscovery of the gospel, recapturing the kerygmatic essence of Christianity. It is, in my estimation, the genius of Christianity that the acknowledgment of this kerygma and the understanding of it are not absolutely dependent upon one particular conception of the nature of the Bible. The dynamic quality of the gospel is likely to break through even when the cast from which it escapes is clearly distinguishable from it and susceptible to a contrast at most every point. Thus Calvin, with his literalistic, supernatural conception of the Bible and also with his absolute confidence in his own interpretation of it, yet penetrated to the basic meaning of the Christian faith. He labored under the assumption that his understanding of faith and his understanding of the Bible were inextricably bound together, and he underlined this conviction by claiming a single theory for the achievement of faith and the correct exegesis of the Bible. The point of this essay, however, is that the two motifs are distinguishable in this theology to such an extent that the one is dependent in no way upon the other.

The danger in Calvin's system, latent for the most part, but occasionally dominant, issuing in regrettable situations, is that, following the assumption that the two are inseparably bound together, a possible result is that the understanding of faith might be obscured with the emphasis on a necessary cognitive content derivable from the scriptures. This might develop into an excessively legalistic and stifling ethic which obscures the freedom of the Christian life or into an excessively dogmatic and stifling theology which obscures the immediacy of the faith relation. Both dangers may be illustrated in later Calvinism.

Later Calvinism, for the most part, fastened on the more rigid and objective motif in Calvin's conception of authority. In the Calvinist orthodoxy of the seventeenth century, verbal inspiration was insisted upon, with no counterbalancing factor. Although Calvin himself had not given an independent discussion to the mode of inspiration in the Bible, most of the Calvinist confessions insisted upon literal dictation by the Holy Spirit. Even the vowel points in the Hebrew text were taken by some to be holy. This put into the hands of the theologians a book which was to be handled almost exclusively as inerrant information about the divine scheme. This contributed to a further development of the role of reason in Calvin's theology. A kind of Protestant scholasticism was created, complete with natural theology and Aristotelian logic. Now the movement was in the direction of an ordering of Christian knowledge far more closely reasoned than that achieved by Calvin.

The result was a series of closed systems of theology, ethics, and polity resting squarely on propositions derived from the Bible and cemented together by an irrefutable logic. So tight were these systems and so clean was their logic that there was no room for movement. The resulting certainty was apparently unshakable. Such was the case in New England, where the clergy was buttressed by "the plain law of the Bible." If a difference of opinion arose, there was great confidence in the ability of the clergy to "persuade" the dissenter. If persuasion did not work, then the only alternative was to judge that the dissenter was sinning against his own conscience.

A partial exception to this development of Calvinism is in English Puritanism, where an emphasis on the Holy Spirit and the day-by-day experience of the Christian unleashed forces which in turn were uncontrollable. This along with numerous other factors created a proliferation of religious movements issuing in the left-wing sects of the revolutionary period and ultimately in Quakerism. For the most part, however, later Calvinism culminated in a static dogmatic comparable with that in New England. It died because of the intransigence brought on by its rigid insistence on the Bible as the authoritative source of knowledge.

Later Calvinism presents a one-sided illustration of the dangers inherent in Calvin's conception of authority. Our study, however, is also instructive for the contemporary situation. It should be realized that the statement of a conception of authority does not answer the problem. The test of any such conception will always come with the barrage of questions like those which have been posed to Calvin's view. What precisely does this conception mean? What are its implications? Is the language involved in it univocal, or, if it is equivocal, is this equivocacy acknowledged and carefully explained? What are the character and the content of the knowledge derived from the authority?

In the present day an additional question must be raised: Does the knowledge derived from the authority meet the criteria for the particular kind of knowledge it claims to be? Although this is perhaps the most troublesome question of the present day, one cannot expect theologians to be willing to submit to the prevailing criteria. Of course, one may have recourse to the supernatural, which issues in a knowledge claimed to be legitimate despite the fact that it is beyond verification or falsification. However, when this is done, the theologian must be aware of what he is about and be quite clear about it.

Where the authority of the Bible is stressed, all of these questions point to the central problem of considering the Bible as a book of knowledge. From our study of Calvin we must gather that it is highly questionable if one can take the whole Bible as such.

Calvin tried to do so, but, as we have seen, he ran into difficulties in relation to both the work of the Spirit and the concrete extraction of the knowledge from the word. It is a tenuous task to compare a historical figure with a contemporary phenomenon, but in the present day those who are perhaps most comparable to Calvin (albeit probably somewhat to his right) are the so-called American "fundamentalists" or "conservatives."

This wing of American Protestantism stands heir primarily to the predominant motifs of Calvinist orthodoxy and to the more objective elements in Calvin's theology. Although the theologians of this group do occasionally speak of the personal character of faith and its self-validating quality, yet the dominant persons in the group are ill at ease in the radical personal language of other theologians and their central emphasis on the essential kerygma. Directly related to this is the preoccupation with a rationalism which must consider everything as matter-of-fact knowledge. This group holds that "revelation is inscripturated, that the Scriptures are the divine provision of the Word of God written."[1] This is the central thesis which determines all theological and apologetic efforts. This means that "revelation is not merely dynamic, but is propositional, and consequently involves revealed truth."[2]

E. J. Carnell also states the position succinctly: "By special revelation we mean not part nor piece, but the full and whole sixty-six canonical books which make up the Bible. . . . These specific books make up the Christian's major premise, since, when added to or subtracted from, one is left with a less coherent world-view than if the manipulation is not undertaken."[3] This statement also introduces us to another interest of the "conservatives." They will be happy with nothing less than a complete world view, through which they believe themselves to have possession of certain knowledge of the divine plan in all its dimensions. It was a part of the divine plan to give this to men, and so the Bible is the organ he chose in which to make clear all that he was about. It is understandable that one who is intent upon precisely clear, factual knowledge of this variety would be driven to a doctrine of verbal infallibility.

It is not that there are no errors in the text. Some have inevitably crept in through its transmission, but those passages "in which the Bible claims to have been originally inerrant" have been shown by the lower critics to be exact. "There is no conjecture at this point. Lower criticism is an exact science."[4] This assertion is subject to question, and it is doubtful if lower criticism meets the general criteria for an exact science. More serious for this position is the doubt that the knowledge derived from the Bible meets the criteria of objective knowledge. Despite the strong emphasis on rational justification, the proponents of this view must, in the last analysis, depend on an acceptance through belief, which in turn calls forth an authority of the character predominating in the theology of Calvin. The issue is a situation in which the believer's response is primarily marked by credulity and docility.

More serious still is the task which faces those who want to take the Bible in this way. Is it possible to hold the view that the Bible is a deposit from heaven, to do justice to every part of it, and to develop a system that is clear, coherent, and lacking in inner contradictions? Certainly this has never been demonstrated, and the mammoth proportions of such a work are staggering. We can only call attention to the problems observable in Calvin's work and claim that anyone proposing a similar position must at least avoid them.

Whatever may be said about the conservative statement, it is at least clear. There is no doubt about what is meant. This must be a criterion for any contemporary statement of authority. Although it may be helpful in many ways, if it is not clear it cannot stand for what it intends to be. The theological work of Karl Barth has been extremely stimulating, and theologians of practically all camps have found it suggestive. His conception of authority, however, may be criticized for its lack of clarity.

It would be unfair to imply that Barth's theology is largely obscure. Quite obviously it has been understood by many, and Barth's place in initiating a theological revival in the twentieth century is undeniable. His major theme is unmistakable to anyone who reads his work seriously, and it is repeated with remarkable persistence. Barth has led Protestant theology to a new appreciation of the transcendence of God and the sin of man, producing a theology radically centered in Jesus Christ as God's act of grace. The focus by Barth on the acting God gives to his words a dramatic and dynamic quality which cannot fail to impress the reader. The transcendent God is he who encounters a man in his personal existence. Barth understands God as a person who works in men here and now. God is a speaking God—a theme important to the Reformers and one for which Barth is severely criticized by the American conservatives, who prefer to say only that God has spoken. For Barth God's word is not "a truth." Rather "it is the truth because it is God's person speaking. . . . It is not something objective, because it is the subjective, namely, God's subjective."[5] "The Word of God is an act of God which happens *specialissime,* in this way and in no other, to this and that particular man."[6]

In his discussion of the authority of the Bible Barth employs language quite consistent with the above. "The problem of the Word of God consists in the fact that to this particular man to-day through the proclamation of this other particular man by means of this particular Bible text this particular manifestation of God is imparted, that a particular *illic et tunc* (then and there) becomes a particular *hic et nunc* (here and now)."[7] Barth distinguishes the Bible from revelation. The Bible only attests the revelation; it is not itself the revelation. "Why and in what respect does the Biblical witness possess authority? It possesses authority in that it claims no authority whatsoever for itself, that its witness amounts to letting the Something else be the authority, itself and by its own agency. Therefore we do the Bible a poor honour, and one unwelcome to itself, when we directly identify it with this something else, with revelation itself."[8] God's speaking and the speaking of a particular biblical author are two different things, although when the Word of God is heard in faith these two become one and the same. Nevertheless revelation is the superior and the Bible the subordinate principle.[9] Without difficulty Barth affirms in principle the historico-critical study of the Bible.

Biblical authority, therefore, is explained dialectically: it is all a matter of No and Yes. He takes humanity-divinity as his symbol, and he uses it literally as well as analogically. Two things, he writes, we must keep before us: "The limitation and the positive element, its distinctiveness from revelation, in so far as it is only a human word about it, and its unity with it, in so far as revelation is the basis, object and content of this word."[10] The Bible is "like the unity of God and man in Jesus Christ."[11] The only difference is that the humanity of scripture is to be distinguished from the glorified humanity of Jesus.[12] It is, in other words, humanly fallible. This fallibility is to be seen not only in the fact that as witness it is not in itself the revelation or that we cannot look at the Bible as a compend of all knowledge, but also in the fact that it has a capacity for error that reaches even to its theological content.[13]

In spite of this concession the Bible is divinely infallible and therefore directly identified with the word of God. This is why it constitutes itself as the canon and why it is the canon just because it is so.[14] Although in one place Barth writes, "The Bible is God's Word so far as God lets it be His Word, so far as God speaks through it,"[15] in another place he claims, "Scripture is recognised as the Word of God by the fact that it *is* the Word of God."[16] Nonetheless it cannot be said that "the Word of God is tied to the Bible." Rather it must be said that "the Bible is tied to the Word of God."[17]

If we take this dialectic to mean that although the Bible is a human book its human writers give the normative witness to God's grace and mercy, particularly in the acts connected with Jesus Christ, then the Yes and No language can be made to yield at least a modicum of understanding. The historical study of the Bible can proceed to clarify this human witness to God's grace, and apparent inconsistencies and obscure passages can be dealt with forthrightly. On the basis of an understanding of the faith of the writers of the Bible, the gospel may be proclaimed with the hope that the faith of *that* age might be kindled in *this* age. Such an application of Barth's language limits the scope of the Bible to human apprehensions of the acts of God (i.e., to interpretations in faith of events in human life), gives the interpreter a guide in determining the pattern of exegesis, and implies nothing with regard to esoteric knowledge about the supernatural order.

But this is not how Barth's language is to be understood. The above explanation is not consistent with Barth's understanding of the divinity of scripture. The No does not affect the Yes in quite this manner. All formulations of the faith, he makes clear, including his own, are relative authorities; Barth prefers to call them spiritual authorities. The Church and the Fathers have only a formal, relative authority under the word.[18] "This means there can never be a final word, but only a word which is imperative and binding and authoritative until it is succeeded by something else."[19] Barth, however, acts as if all this were not the case. The Church confession is not final, but yet it must be made in full certainty. He quotes with approval Luther's absolute statement about the articles of Schmalcald.[20] If this is the case with the authority of the Church, then in the discussion of the authority of the Bible he is all the more certain. With Barth this certainty goes beyond certainty as a correlate of trust in God's grace through Jesus Christ and becomes also a certainty with regard to the truth of the Bible as a whole. Barth does not want to assume a position from which he controls the Bible,[21] but in his anxiety to be controlled by it he surrenders his critical stance and accepts the statements of knowledge through which the faith is expressed as well as the faith itself. Symptomatic of this is his uncritical acceptance of the virgin birth.

In his dialectic Barth takes account of the historical nature of the scripture, but it is doubtful if he actually takes this historical character seriously in his exegesis, particularly when that is based on the method of *pneumatikos pneumatika*,[22] an appeal to the Spirit which faces the same difficulties noted in Chapter V in the case of Calvin, namely, those involving the discernment of the Spirit. It is Barth's basic position that the text of the Bible must be taken seriously in discussing theological issues, but because of his dialectic he has no ascertainable guide.

After the Amsterdam meeting of the World Council of Churches Reinhold Niebuhr and Karl Barth engaged in an exchange of articles in the *Christian Century* magazine in which the question of the Bible was discussed. Barth complained that the Anglo-Saxon theologians cried "literalist" when he suggested that the Commission on the Word of Women should refer to I Corinthians 11 and Ephesians 5 (enjoining women to be subject to their husbands and the former also instructing women not to pray with unveiled heads) as well as to Galatians 3 ("There is neither male nor female; for you are all one in Christ Jesus").[23] Niebuhr countered: "I am informed that Barth dismissed the authority of the Pauline injunction that women must not pray in the church with the head uncovered. He regarded that injunction as 'time bound.' But as far as I know he did not give a criterion for determining what is time bound and what is timeless in these scriptural injunctions."[24] This is the problem encountered by a dialectic such as Barth has outlined, and we have seen that Calvin encountered analogous difficulties in the interpretation of scripture.

His dialectic, the No and the Yes, is comprehensible so long as he is focusing on the events of God's grace and especially the understanding of Jesus Christ as the supreme event. In those instances the No is seen as the natural, the human aspect with no obvious meaning, while the Yes is the meaning given the event by faith. The No is the human statement in the Bible which has no support universally acknowledged by human capacities (reason, matter-of-fact evidence, etc.), and it becomes the Yes when faith in the divine meaning is evoked in the one who reads or hears. But when this dialectic is transferred to other statements in the Bible (such as injunctions about women) the meaning of the dialectic is obscured. The No is abrogated, and the Yes is affirmed arbitrarily. One is then in a position of having to take all parts seriously as decrees having divine sanctions, and if he should chose to moderate any part or perhaps reject something he does so with no clear guide.

The transition from a Yes with regard to what has to do with faith in the grace of God in Christ to a Yes with reference to statements about other matters not clearly related to God's gracious deeds is not apparent. Once it is made, however, the interpreter will be interested in finding the meaning of the whole, and he will be uneasy in the face of a passage whose meaning is difficult to ascertain. This may be seen in Barth's Christological interpretation of the Old Testament. He feels quite impelled to find Christ proclaimed throughout the Old Testament by means of types and figures. An illustration of this is Barth's treatment of Leviticus 14 and 16. Chapter 14 deals with legislation regarding leprosy, itches, and other skin disorders, while chapter 16 presents the regulations governing the sin offerings and the Day of Atonement. Barth devotes a number of pages to the interpretation of these chapters and reaches the climax with these words: "Either the subject of the Old Testament witness is an unknown quantity [and this, he says, would mean that "the Old Testament as a whole has no subject, that its witness points into the void"] . . . Or the subject of the Old Testament witness is identical with the person of Jesus Christ."[25] Shortly after this he declares, "Whoever intends to deny this as the last word of exegesis on Lev. 14 and 16 will either have to set out upon the proof of another, better last word in explanation of these texts, or he must acknowledge that he does not know one, that he therefore does not finally know of whom or what these texts speak."[26] One observes the implication that it is a serious weakness to admit ignorance about the subject of these texts (assuming that it is something besides ancient priestly regulations about skin diseases and atonement sacrifices). In spite of the fact that Barth's interpretation here augments his Christocentrism, it is a Christocentrism different from that which interprets Christian faith radically in the light of Jesus Christ as the supreme act of God's grace and stops there. The former does not deny the latter, but in going beyond it, it requires a sacrifice of the intellect insofar as there is no evidence whatever that the priestly writers of the Old Testament intended to set forth a figure of Jesus Christ. The latter, which, of course, does not imply the former, requires no sacrifice of the intellect because it is based on a historical understanding of the writers who do talk about Jesus as the Christ. It is then content to understand such Old Testament passages historically also and experiences no embarrassment if it must say that the significance for salvation of such passages, if there is any, is not apparent.

It cannot be said that Barth avoids the dangers of literalism by his appreciation of the Bible as a whole and as a unity and by his central emphasis on the kerygma and on Christ. Contemporary theology is deeply indebted to Barth for having called to the

Church's attention again the essential nature of its proclamation, but when Barth, whose mind must be driven by an undaunting curiosity and a deep craving for knowledge, pushes on beyond the kerygma to declare in his *Dogmatik* what apparently is everything about everything in the Christian religion, and when he can lecture in full seriousness for a year on the angels, it must be admitted that he is using the Bible—dialectically we must assume—to enlighten men on all sorts of knowledge, which, although it is never certain, must nevertheless be asserted and proclaimed as if there were no other truth at all.

Rudolph Bultmann's theological approach is to be commended, at least for the forthrightness and clarity with which he tackles the problem of authority. He bases it consistently in personal faith and claims significance for theological statements only insofar as they are related to personal faith. Bultmann is interested in saying only one thing, and that, to my mind, has been best summarized by Friedrich Gogarten in his little book on the demythologizing controversy. He writes that demythologization (and I should like to add, the whole of Bultmann's work) "aims at enabling modern thought simply to know once again what Christian faith involves."[27]

If this is the single aim of Bultmann's work, then the validity of that work hinges upon his exclusive use of the *erga nos, pro me* (toward us, for me) theme in the thought of the Reformers. Melanchthon's classic statement of this theme appears on numerous occasions in Bultmann's theological writings: "This is to know Christ, to know his benefits, not to contemplate his natures or the mode of his incarnation." The similarity of this statement to statements by Calvin on the meaning of faith at the beginning of Book III in the *Institutes* is unmistakable.

Since this is Bultmann's basic interest, he is consistent when he insists that no faith can be authentic which demands of the believer a surrender of the understanding. "Christian preaching, in so far as it is preaching of the Word of God by God's command and in His name, does not offer a doctrine which can be accepted . . . by a *sacrificium intellectus*."[28] If a man believes something without understanding what he believes, then that belief is arbitrary. Any benefits derived from such a belief would be dependent on some almost magical working, as if a man could change his own state of affairs by a word, even if he didn't know the meaning of that word. Certainly such a belief is heteronomous, and the man himself can hardly be a part of his faith. Just because it is not understood it cannot become the focal point determining his entire life. The term "understanding" is probably the most frequently used word in Bultmann's vocabulary. But what is entailed in understanding when its object is faith? To understand faith is to know in one's own personal history the benefits of Christ, as Melanchthon and Calvin indicate.

Bultmann regularly makes use of analogies taken from personal relationships to clarify this point. Take love, for example. One can observe the phenomena of love, see what it does, submit it to tests to learn things about it, but it is doubtful if one could ever come to understand what love is by this method. As Bultmann puts it, "The love of my friend, my wife, my children, meets me genuinely only here and now as an event. Such love cannot be observed by objective methods but only by personal experience and response. From the outside, for example, by psychological observation, it cannot be perceived as love, but only as an interesting detail of psychological processes which are open to different interpretations."[29] One understands love only when he himself loves or understands himself to be loved.

The analogy is instructive with regard to Bultmann's mode of talking about God. No amount of objective knowledge about God (passing for the moment the question of the validity of such knowledge) is tantamount to understanding God. God is only understood when a man acknowledges God's working in his own life and through his own act of will gives his life over to be determined by God.

"*Works* of love are fundamentally easy even when I extort them from myself in certain circumstances with an effort; for in them I remain my old self. The real *act* of love is fundamentally difficult and is not to be extorted by any violence, as I give away myself in it, and attain my being only by losing it in this act."[30] Let us paraphrase this statement: So-called objective knowledge of God is fundamentally easy and can be deduced simply by an effort of my mind, for in this I remain my old self—nothing about me is called into question. To understand God is to call into question my previous self-understanding and to understand myself anew, namely as dependent in every respect upon God, as living by his Spirit and receiving new life through his grace. This takes the place of a previous self-understanding, the supposition that I am able to live by my own powers. To know God is simultaneously to know myself. To speak of God is simultaneously to speak of myself.

In relation to the Bible Bultmann sees this as an explanation of Paul's teaching on justification by faith. Justification is an act of God, not an eternal principle in the structure of the Godhead. It does not convey "enlightenment" as if it were an unknown concept which now reveals the interconnectedness of a vast complex of ideas. Moreover, to Bultmann's way of thinking it is not the proclamation of an *idea* about God telling us that God's disposition is really gracious rather than wrathful. On the contrary, justification is God's deed which can be apprehended not from a neutral or objective point of observation but only as we understand that it happens to ourselves. This involves a new self-understanding.[31]

Bultmann views man essentially as a historical being. Life is not some static quintessential substance subject to disinterested analysis. Rather the locus of life is a man's actions and reactions in his own situation. Man is "an historical being not only in so far as he is enmeshed in the course of world-history, but particularly in so far as he has a personal history of his own."[32] Faith in God is faith in One who is effective in this historical existence. To speak of God is to speak at the same time of oneself, and to speak of Christ is to speak at the same time of one's salvation. Theology is simultaneously anthropology, and christology is simultaneously soteriology.[33] "This is to know Christ, to know his benefits."

Having observed Bultmann's category for understanding faith, we are now in a position to draw out the implications for his conception and use of the Bible. One thing should be immediately clear: He cannot conceive the Bible as authoritative in any objective way. It is not a divine deposit of truths intended to guide man's otherwise misdirected mind through the maze of confusing data. When the basis for the authority of the Bible rests on its givenness, its objectivity, this authority has no intrinsic relation to one's self-understanding. Any significance that such an authority could muster for one's concrete historical life would be a derived significance, not an immediate one.

As one reads Bultmann's writings one begins to think that the question of authority is to him a pseudo-problem. In a generation when most theologians write a good deal about the problem, Bultmann has devoted no one writing to this question exclusively. This observation is symptomatic. The Bible is authoritative to Bultmann in a certain sense, but he views the question of authority as secondary to a much larger problem—the question of hermeneutics, of interpretation.

Most simply (and this is misleading until it is fully explained), the Bible is authoritative insofar as it conveys that understanding of Christian faith which has constituted the Church. Thus, whenever a man wants to know what the Christian faith is about, he must begin with the Bible. If this is the case, then he who seeks to understand what that faith was is under the most rigorous compulsion to recover the authentic record insofar as that is possible. Just this conviction has been responsible for Bultmann's specifically historico-critical studies. For Bultmann the passion for rigorous criticism rises precisely from the desire to study the Bible with all seriousness. Once a man has rejected the view of the Bible as an objective, unquestionable authority, he is impelled to approach the Bible with a finely honed historical scalpel.

More than this, however, is involved if one is to take the Bible as the normative source for understanding Christian faith. After one has tackled the critical problems, one faces the real task: understanding the early conception of faith. Here arises the problem of hermeneutics, of interpreting what is said in the Bible. If Bultmann is somewhat unusual in that he has written nothing specifically on the subject of authority, he is also somewhat unusual in the amount of attention he has given to the general problem of hermeneutics. His method of interpretation fits into the general pattern of his thought as we have followed it up to this point.

If one is to understand Jesus, for example, one must focus

upon what Jesus himself purposed, but this means to focus upon "what in his purpose as a part of history makes a present demand upon us."[34] This, however, involves posing a particular set of questions to the texts in advance. The questions have to do with one's own understanding of life and destiny, of God and man; and, to be sure, they suggest a previous understanding (Bultmann's much discussed *Vorverständnis*). This previous understanding, however, is no sweeping assertion of natural, inborn knowledge of God. It is merely the observation that every man, consciously or unconsciously, has questions about his own personal existence, his personal history. And as Bultmann puts it, in many places, in many ways, "The question of God and the question of myself are identical."[35]

This previous understanding (these questions which are put to the text at hand) is only methodological; it has nothing to do with the results of the investigation. Indeed, by bringing it to the consciousness one is much more likely to allow it to be affected by the text rather than letting it determine the results of the exegesis. Furthermore, according to Bultmann, a good case can be made for speaking of this as the most objective possible approach. If the object of one's investigation of a particular text is the understanding of life enshrined in it, then it stands to reason that "only those who are stirred by the question of their own existence can hear the claim which the text makes."[36] Hermeneutics may have any one of a number of possible objects, but where it is interested in understanding the conception of human life in a document it "presupposes the utmost liveness of the comprehending subject, and the richest possible unfolding of his individuality."[37]

In the case of Jesus, then, one must focus on his teachings because he worked primarily through the medium of the word. But here again, his teachings are not understood as general truths which have validity apart from the consideration of time. "The ideas are understood in the light of the concrete situation of a man living in time; as his interpretation of his own existence in the midst of change, uncertainty, decision; as the expression of a possibility of comprehending this life; as the effort to gain clear insight into the contingencies and necessities of his own existence.

When we encounter the words of Jesus in history, *we* do not judge *them* by a philosophical system with reference to their rational validity; *they* meet *us* with the question of how we are to interpret our own existence. That we be ourselves deeply disturbed by the problem of our own life is therefore the indispensable condition of our inquiry."[38]

We can now see in what terms Bultmann is willing to speak of the Bible as authoritative: The Bible is authoritative only insofar as it communicates the claim (*Anspruch*) of God on me and thus leads me to radical obedience in faith. It is authoritative insofar as it calls into question my previous self-understanding and leads me to a new self-understanding—from seeing myself as a person who must and perhaps can make his own way to seeing myself as a sinner before God who by God's now occurring act of grace has been given new life with an openness to the future. If the word "authority" is inappropriate to this conception, we shall do without it. As a matter of fact, Bultmann seldom uses the word. Slightly more often he uses the term "revelation." But even this word is inappropriate except when one conceives it as happening only when it is apprehended by a man in his concrete history. The decisive acts of God are actually spoken of in two tenses by Bultmann. The events of salvation are historically past; they occurred in the historical figure Jesus of Nazareth. In another sense they are present. That is, they are contemporary to the man who apprehends them as the events of his salvation, and insofar as this apprehension means the reversal of one's self-understanding, the events have occurred again in the believer's own history.

The value of Bultmann's work is that, in effect, he turns Calvin around. We saw that Calvin, in his conception of authority, spoke most strongly for the Bible as objective authority demanding from the believer obedience and docility. Within this framework an understanding of the meaning of the gospel and the nature of faith was not only possible but was eloquently stated. However, because of the foundation of the conception of authority certain problems and consequent dangers inevitably developed. Whatever may be the limitations of his theological work as a whole, Bultmann points Christian theology in a relatively unexplored direction by claiming a radical precedence for faith which he understands in a way not uncongenial to Calvin. The consistent centrality of personal faith sets up boundaries for the authority of scripture. Here it is not that the belief in the Bible as containing correct knowledge produces an understanding of faith, a situation in which the point of beginning carries with it a number of things which can be defended only by an appeal to obedience and docility, and even then uneasily. The understanding of faith cannot be independent of the Bible, but when one makes faith the basis of the conception of authority, the biblical material can be assimilated—not uncritically—in such a way that the *erga nos* (toward us) is present and determinative throughout. As a result, not only is theology unified but the man of faith is unified, and he is able to give himself totally in heart, mind, soul, and strength in his theology.

This mode of theology contributes to the solution of the perplexing problem of the nonpermanence of theological systems. Theological formulations are not fundamental. They should be no more than the stammering efforts of men to explore the implications of the one thing in the Christian faith which has been constant since its beginning. The passing away of a system should not entail in any way a weakening of the underpinning. That remains secure so long as a man is convicted of the gratuitous mercy of God toward him. This approach would serve to bring theology closer to those nontheologians who sometimes have a firmer grasp of the meaning of faith than do the theologians themselves, and it would assist the theologian in understanding that this phenomenon is not a mystery or a paradox.

Doing the work of theology consistently from this foundation would perhaps entail the surrender of a large block of what has previously been taken as knowledge of God and his plan. It would at least involve a careful (and different) description of the character of knowledge. It would, at the same time, distinguish the work of the theologian from the metaphysician and protect him from the justified jeers of those who stand on the outside, incredulous at the theologians' flagrant violations of scientific norms and plain facts. The theologian needs to be saved from concupiscence in respect to knowledge of divine things. This may, perhaps, best be accomplished by facing squarely the criteria for knowledge and by assessing boldly the importance and significance of much that has been claimed for knowledge in the past.

An effective way to come by such a conception of authority as we have been discussing is through a careful study of John Calvin. In this way many of the problems and a number of the insights deriving from a consideration of the Bible as authoritative may be seen. One can take heart in the discovery that out of the rather rigid cast of Calvin's theology a clear understanding of faith arises even as a semi-independent authority in itself, but one can still be made aware of the dangers: the possibilities that faith might be even partially obscured and its structure of authority weakened. The task which always confronts the theologian, especially with regard to the problem of authority, is to find that basis for theology most conducive to the full understanding of faith and least likely to obscure faith's meaning. The foundation is that which requires the most certain and stable construction.

Notes

The footnote references to Calvin's works are abbreviated in order to give the fullest reference in a small space. They are so constructed that the reader can readily find the references either in translation or in the original language. The notes normally consist of two sets of symbols. The first is general so that the reference can be located in any edition. The second points more specifically to the source in the original language. A reference to a passage in the *Institutes* is: II. i. 8 (O.S. III. 238.11–15). The passage will be found in Book II, Chapter i, paragraph 8. In the Latin it may be located in *Calvini opera selecta*, Volume III, page 238, lines 11–15. A reference to a passage from the commentaries is: Com. Ezek. 12:4–6 (C.O. 40.256). The passage may be found in any edition of the Commentary on Ezekiel in the comments on chapter 12, verses 4–6, of that book. The Latin will be found in *Ioannis Calvini opera quae supersunt omnia*, Volume 40, column 256. In the case of references which are not numbered in translation by paragraph or verse the specific page reference in an English translation is given.

Chapter I

[1] *Jean Calvin: Les hommes et les choses de son temps*, p. 60.
[2] I. i. 1 (O.S. III. 31.1–3).   [3] I. i. 1 (O.S. III. 31.17–18).   [4] I. i. 1 (O.S. III. 31.28–32.1).   [5] I. i. 1 (O.S. III. 31.21–32.2).   [6] I. i. 1 (O.S. III. 32.7–9).   [7] I . i. 2 (O.S. III. 32.10–18).   [8] II. i. 1 (O.S. III. 228.20–28).   [9] II. i. 8 (O.S. III. 236.33–237.2).   [10] II. i. 8 (O.S. III. 238.11–15).
[11] II. ii. 10 (O.S. III. 252.20f).   [12] I. ii. 1 (O.S. III. 35.5–8).   [13] I. ii. 2 (O.S. III. 35.20–24).   [14] See I. v (O.S. III. 44–60).   [15] I. v. 11 (O.S. III. 55.3–6).   [16] I. v. 13 (O.S. III. 57–58).   [17] Com. Phil. 1:29 (C.O. 52.22).   [18] III. ii. 3 (O.S. IV. 11.3–8).   [19] I. xiv. 1 (O.S. III. 152.10).   [20] I. xiv. 1 (O.S. III. 153.5–7).
[21] II. ii. 21 (O.S. III. 264.15–20).   [22] I. xiii. 1 (O.S. III. 109.-11–18).   [23] I. vi. 1 (O.S. III. 60.25–30).   [24] I. vi. 2 (O.S. III.

62.8–10).   [25] I. vi. 3 (O.S. III. 63.15–20).   [26] Com. Jer. 15:18 (C.O. 38.231).   [27] Com. Gen. 17:4 (C.O. 23.236).   [28] *Ibid.* [29] Com. II Tim. 3:16 (C.O. 52.383).   [30] Com. II Tim. 3:16 (C.O. 52.383).

[31] Com. Hosea 1:2 (C.O. 42.203).   [32] See Com. I Peter 1:12 (C.O. 55.219).   [33] III. ii. 35 (O.S. IV. 46.1).   [34] Com. Jn. 6:65 (C.O. 47.161).   [35] III. ii. 34 (O.S. IV. 45.33–38).   [36] I. vii. 4 (O.S. III. 69.7–11).   [37] I. viii. 13 (O.S. III. 81.23–25).   [38] III. ii. 33 (O.S. IV. 44.4–19).   [39] I. vii. 5 (O.S. III. 70.16–30).   [40] Com. II Tim. 3:16 (C.O. 52.283).

[41] Com. Jn. 15:27 (C.O. 47.354).   [42] I. ix. 3 (O.S. III. 84.35–38).   [43] Dedication to the *Institutes,* the Open Letter to Francis I (Allen, p. 23; O.S. III. 12.9–11).   [44] Dedication to the *Institutes* (Allen, pp. 23–24; O.S. III. 12.25–13.1).

Chapter II

[1] Preface to the *Institutes,* Allen, pp. 18–19 (O.S. III. 6.18–24). [2] Com. Jn. 16:13 (C.O. 47.361–62).   [3] Com. Ps. 25:14 (C.O. 31.-259).   [4] IV. viii. 7 (O.S. V. 139.22–28).   [5] III. xxv. 10 (O.S. IV. 453.28–29).   [6] III. xxi. 2 (O.S. IV. 371.9ff).   [7] III. xxi. 3 (O.S. IV. 371.34ff).   [8] Com. II. Tim. 3:15 (C.O. 52.382).   [9] Dedication to the *Institutes,* Allen, p. 28 (O.S. III. 17.18–20).   [10] *Ibid.* (O.S. III. 17.22).

[11] *Ibid.* (O.S. III. 17.30–18.3).   [12] I. xiii. 19 (O.S. III. 133.-23).   [13] IV. ix. 8 (O.S. V. 156.34–35).   [14] IV. ix. 1 (O.S. V. 151.8–11); IV. ix. 2 (O.S. V. 151.28–30; 152.2–7).   [15] IV. ix. 9 (O.S. V. 157.16–17).   [16] I. xiii. 3 (O.S. III. 111–12).   [17] II. xvi. 18 (O.S. III. 506.24–31).   [18] *Reply to Sadolet,* in *Calvin: Theological Treatises,* p. 255 (C.O. 5.415).   [19] Dedication to the *Institutes,* Allen, pp. 20–22 (O.S. III. 9–12).   [20] *Ibid.,* p. 23 (O.S. III. 12.20–23).

[21] Com. Joshua 7:24 (C.O. 25.479–80).   [22] IV. i. 3 (O.S. V. 6.9–11).   [23] IV. i. 2 (O.S. V. 2.5–17).   [24] IV. i. 3 (O.S. V. 4.20–5.2).   [25] IV. i. 4 (O.S. V. 7.5–11).   [26] IV. i. 20 (O.S. V. 24.3–4).   [27] IV. xii. 4 (O.S. V. 214.26–215.2).   [28] IV. iii. 1 (O.S. V. 42.20–29).   [29] IV. i. 6 (O.S. V. 11.8–9).   [30] IV. i. 9 (O.S. V. 13.23–27).

[31] IV. viii. 13 (O.S. V. 146.25–31).   [32] IV. viii. 2 (O.S. V. 134.-17–18).   [33] IV. viii. 9 (O.S. V. 141.17–19); IV. viii. 15 (O.S. V. 149.16–20).   [34] I. vii. 1 (O.S. III. 66.12–15).   [35] IV. viii. 15 (O.S. V. 149.19–20).   [36] IV. viii. 9 (O.S. V. 141.11–16).   [37] III. xvi. 4 (O.S. IV. 252.32–34).   [38] III. vi. 1 (O.S. IV. 146.17–21).

[39] III. vi. 1 (O.S. IV. 147.16–19). [40] I. iii. 1 (O.S. III. 37–38);
I. v. 3 (O.S. III. 47.3–6); I. v. 13 (O.S. III. 57).
[41] I. i. 3 (O.S. III. 33). [42] I. ix. 1 (O.S. III. 82.20–21).
[43] Com. Jn. 5:46 (C.O. 47.129). [44] I. v. 7 (O.S. III. 52.1–9).
[45] I. v. 8 (O.S. III. 52–53). [46] II. x. 12 (O.S. III. 412.34–35).
[47] II. x. 13 (O.S. III. 414); cf. Com. Heb. 11 (C.O. 55.143ff).
[48] II. xi. 1 (O.S. III. 424.7–9). [49] II. xi. 2 (O.S. III. 424–25).
[50] I. xvii. 4 (O.S. III. 207.19–21).
[51] I. xvii. 5 (O.S. III. 208). [52] II. iv. 2 (O.S. III. 292. 5–8).
[53] II. iv. 2 (O.S. III. 292.19–29). [54] II. iv. 3 (O.S. III. 292.33–34).
[55] Com. II Tim. 3:16 (C.O. 52.384).

Chapter III

[1] I. i. 1 (O.S. III. 31.1–3). [2] Com. Jn. 15:18 (C.O. 47.349).
[3] Com. Jn. 9:7 (C.O. 47.221–22). [4] Com. Jn. 14:31 (C.O. 47.338).
[5] Com. John, Argument (C.O. 47.vii). [6] III. ii. [7] III. ii. 7 (O.S.
IV. 15.19–21). [8] III. ii. 7 (O.S. IV. 15.24–28). [9] III. ii. 13
(O.S. IV. 23.31–32; 24.6, 14–17, 20–21, 27–30). [10] III. ii. 29
(O.S. IV. 39.1–6).
[11] III. ii. 30 (O.S. IV. 40.9–12). [12] Com. Acts 16:31–32 (C.O.
48.389).

Chapter IV

[1] Cf. J. K. S. Reid, *The Authority of Scripture,* pp. 36ff; Wilhelm
Niesel, *The Theology of Calvin,* pp. 35ff. [2] Benjamin B. Warfield,
Calvin and Calvinism, pp. 63–64. Cf. Edward A. Dowey, Jr., *The
Knowledge of God in Calvin's Theology,* pp. 90–105; Brian A. Gerrish, "Biblical Authority and the Continental Reformation," pp. 348–
60. [3] Gerrish, pp. 336–39. [4] II. xvi. 2 (O.S. III. 483.20).
[5] IV. ix. 7 (O.S. V. 155.33–34). [6] Com. Phil. 1:6 (C.O. 52.9).
[7] Com. Col. 1:20 (C.O. 52.89). [8] Com. Gen. 49:10 (C.O. 23.958).
[9] Com. Acts 1:20 (C.O. 48.20). [10] Com. Ezek. 12:4–6 (C.O. 40.-
256).
[11] I. viii. 2 (O.S. III. 73.1–3). [12] Com. Ps. 39:13 (C.O. 31.404–
5). [13] *Ibid.* [14] *Ibid.* [15] Com. Ps. 77, Argument (C.O. 31.711).
[16] Com. Ps. 44:19 (C.O. 31.445). [17] III. xx. 49 (O.S. IV. 365.31–
34). [18] Com. I Peter 1:11 (C.O. 55.217). [19] Com. Daniel, introductory remarks in Lecture I (C.O. 40.530). [20] Com. Ex. 3:1 (C.O.
24.34).

[21] Doumergue, p. 73. [22] Warfield, p. 63. [23] Com. Jer. 44:15 (C.O. 39.260–61). [24] II. vii. 7 (O.S. III. 332). [25] III. ii. 6 (O.S. IV. 14.31–15.1). [26] Peter Brunner, *Vom Glauben bei Calvin*, p. 93. [27] Com. Gen. 3:17 (C.O. 23.73). [28] Com. Eph. 3:10 (C.O. 51.183). [29] I. xiv. 21 (O.S. III. 171.26–30); I. xv. 4 (O.S. III. 179.3–5). [30] Preface to Com. Gal., Eph., Phil., Col. (C.O. 12.659).

[31] II. xiv. 5 (O.S. III. 464.19–465.1). [32] III. xxiv. 5 (O.S. IV. 416.3–4). [33] Com. Ps. 78:3 (C.O. 31.722). [34] Wilhelm Niesel, p. 35. [35] Niesel, p. 31. [36] I. xiii. 3 (O.S. III. 111.20–112.1). [37] I. xiii. 3 (O.S. III. 112.1–5). [38] I. xiii. 14 (O.S. III. 128.9–12). [39] I. xiii. 15 (O.S. III. 129.7–10). [40] Com. Joshua, Argument (C.O. 25.421–22).

[41] Com. Rom. 15:4 (C.O. 49.271). [42] Com. Hosea 14:9 (C.O. 42.512). [43] Com. II Cor. 7:8 (C.O. 50.88). [44] Com. Jn. 5:30 (C.O. 47.121). [45] I. vii. 1 (O.S. III. 65.11–16). [46] I. ix. 2 (O.S. III. 83.33–35). [47] II. xi. 13 (O.S. III. 435.16–19). [48] Com. I Cor. 2:9 (C.O. 49.339). [49] Com. Ps. 32:1 (C.O. 31.315). [50] III. xvii. 11 (O.S. IV. 264.9–12).

[51] III. xvii. 11 (O.S. IV. 264.17, 28–31; 265.2–5). [52] III. xvii. 12 (O.S. IV. 265.27–29). [53] III. xvii. 12 (O.S. IV. 265.27–266.-11). [54] J. K. S. Reid, pp. 41–42. [55] *Ibid.*, pp. 22ff. [56] C.O. 9.285, translated in Niesel, p. 27. [57] C.O. 47.125. Cf. Niesel, p. 27. [58] C.O. 53.560, translated in Niesel, p. 27. [59] C.O. 47.125. [60] Cf. Com. Ps. 19:8 (C.O. 31.200–201). [61] I. ix. 1 (O.S. III. 81–83).

Chapter V

[1] Com. Heb. 8:10 (C.O. 55.102). [2] III. i. 1 (O.S. IV. 1.10–14, 21–24). [3] III. i. 1 (O.S. IV. 1.26–28). [4] III. i. 1 (O.S. IV. 2.5–6). [5] III. i. 3 (O.S. IV. 5.2–4). [6] III. i. 4 (O.S. IV. 5.14–17). [7] III. i. 2 (O.S. IV. 2.11–14). [8] III. i. 3 (O.S. IV. 4.4–5). [9] III. i. 3 (O.S. IV. 4.5–7). [10] III. i. 3 (O.S. IV. 4.16–19).

[11] III. i. 3 (O.S. IV. 4.19–5.1). [12] I. vii. 4 (O.S. III. 69–70). [13] I. vii. 2 (O.S. III. 66.17–18). [14] I. vii. 1 (O.S. III. 66.12–15). [15] I. vii. 3 (O.S. III. 67–68). [16] I. vii. 4 (O.S. III. 69.7–11). [17] I. vii. 4 (O.S. III. 69.25–34). [18] I. vii. 4 (O.S. III. 70.2–3). [19] I. vii. 5 (O.S. III. 70.19). [20] I. vii. 5 (O.S. III. 70.24–27).

[21] I. vii. 5 (O.S. III. 71.12–14). [22] I. vii. 5 (O.S. III. 71.33–35). [23] I. vii. 5 (O.S. III. 71.14–17). [24] III. i. 4 (O.S. IV. 6.3–8). [25] C.O. 32.270. [26] C.O. 37.276. [27] C.O. 32.24. [28] IV. viii. 13 (O.S. V. 147.16–18). [29] Com. Rom. 11:34 (C.O. 49.231). [30] III. ii. 34 (O.S. IV. 45.35–36).

³¹ Com. Jer. 31:19 (C.O. 38.674). ³² Com. Jer. 24:7 (C.O. 38.463). ³³ Com. Jn. 16:25 (C.O. 47.370). ³⁴ Com. Jn. 17:26 (C.O. 47.390). ³⁵ Com. Jn. 6:45 (C.O. 47.149). ³⁶ Com. I Thess. 5:19 (C.O. 52.175). ³⁷ Com. I Cor. 2:14 (C.O. 49.344). ³⁸ Com. II Peter 1:20 (C.O. 55.457). ³⁹ Com. Acts 17:11 (C.O. 48.400–401). ⁴⁰ Com. Acts 8:31 (C.O. 48.192).

⁴¹ *Ibid.* ⁴² IV. iii. 1 (O.S. V. 42.26–28). ⁴³ IV. i. 3 (O.S. V. 6.9–11). ⁴⁴ IV. i. 10 (O.S. V. 14.34–35). ⁴⁵ IV. xii. 4 (O.S. V. 214.26–215.2). ⁴⁶ IV. i. 5 (O.S. V. 9.3–4). ⁴⁷ IV. i. 9 (O.S. V. 13.23–27). ⁴⁸ IV. i. 6 (O.S. V. 11.1–10). ⁴⁹ Com. Jer. 5:13 (C.O. 37.622). ⁵⁰ Com. Micah 3:8 (C.O. 43.329).

⁵¹ Com. Acts 26:18 (C.O. 48.543). ⁵² *Antidote to the Council of Trent*, in *Tracts of Calvin*; note particularly Calvin's Preface to the *Antidote*, III (1851), 32 (C.O. 7.381). ⁵³ C.O. 55.328. ⁵⁴ Com. I Jn. 2:27 (C.O. 55.327–28). ⁵⁵ Com. Matt. 7:16 (C.O. 45.225–27). ⁵⁶ C.O. 31.181–82. ⁵⁷ Com. I Jn. 4:6 (C.O. 55.350–51). ⁵⁸ Dedication to the *Institutes*, Allen, p. 23 (O.S. III. 12.29ff). ⁵⁹ *Antidote*, in *Calvin's Tracts*, III, 35 (C.O. 7.383–84). ⁶⁰ Com. Jn. 5:43 (C.O. 47.127).

⁶¹ Com. Gal. 1:1 (C.O. 50.167). ⁶² Com. I Jn. 4:6 (C.O. 55.-351–52). ⁶³ Com. I Jn. 4:6 (C.O. 55.352). ⁶⁴ Com. Jn. 1:1 (C.O. 47.8). ⁶⁵ Com. Jer. 23:21 (C.O. 38.433). ⁶⁶ Com. Jer. 23:22 (C.O. 38.43); cf. Jer. 29:30–32 (C.O. 38.611). ⁶⁷ C.O. 47.52–53. ⁶⁸ Com. Isa. 61:1 (C.O. 37.371–72). ⁶⁹ Com. Jer. 15:19 (C.O. 38.234). Cf. I. ix. 3 (O.S. III. 84.14–20, 35ff); Jer. 14:13, 14 (C.O. 38.193); Jer. 15:19 (C.O. 38.234); Jer. 23:16 (C.O. 38.426); Com. Matt. 23:2 (C.O. 45.621–23); Com. Jn. 7:48 (C.O. 47.185–86); Com. Acts 17:11 (C.O. 48.401). Each of these passages emphasizes the Bible as the sole criterion in judging a teacher. ⁷⁰ C.O. 55.347.

⁷¹ C.O. 55.348. ⁷² See especially Com. Jer. 2:19 (C.O. 37.-517); Com. Jer. 6:27 (C.O. 37.667); Com. Jer. 9:6 (C.O. 38.31). ⁷³ Com. Phil. 1:6 (C.O. 52.9). ⁷⁴ *Ibid.*

Chapter VI

¹ I. i. 1 (O.S. III. 31.6–8). ² III. ii. 2 (O.S. IV. 10.9–10). ³ III. ii. 2 (O.S. IV. 10.11–12). ⁴ III. ii. 1 (O.S. IV. 6.19–20). ⁵ O.S. IV. 6.3–9, 13. ⁶ III. ii. 1 (O.S. IV. 7.19–21). ⁷ III. ii. 1 (O.S. IV. 7.21–23). ⁸ III. ii. 1 (O.S. IV. 9.9–13). ⁹ III. ii. 6 (O.S. IV. 13.15–18). ¹⁰ III. ii. 6 (O.S. IV. 13.18–20).

¹¹ III. ii. 6 (O.S. IV. 15.6–11). ¹² *The Knowledge of God in Calvin's Theology*, pp. 153–204. ¹³ *Ibid.*, pp. 205ff. ¹⁴ *Ibid.*, p.

205.   [15] *Ibid.*, p. 207.   [16] *The Theology of Calvin,* especially chap.
9.   [17] *The Knowledge of God in Calvin's Theology.*   [18] Com. Dan.
8:15 (C.O. 41.109).   [19] Com. Corinthians, Argument (C.O. 49.-
304).   [20] Com. Jer. 31:34 (C.O. 38.694).

[21] Com. Phil. 1:9 (C.O. 52.12).   [22] I. vi. 2 (O.S. III. 62.1–10).
[23] I. xiv. 1 (O.S. III. 152.4–21).   [24] I. xiv. 1 (O.S. III. 152.15–17).
[25] I. xiv. 20 (O.S. III. 171.15–17).   [26] Com. Gen. 2:10 (C.O.
23.40).   [27] Com. Genesis, Argument (C.O. 23.5–6).   [28] Com.
Joshua 10:13 (C.O. 25.500).   [29] *Ibid.*   [30] Com. Ps. 110:4 (C.O.
32.163).

[31] Com. Jn. 20:5 (C.O. 47.428).   [32] Com. Acts 13:29 (C.O.
48.297–98).   [33] II. viii. 21 (O.S. III. 363.21–23).   [34] II. v. 1
(O.S. III. 298.10–12); cf. II. v. 4 (O.S. III. 301–2).   [35] II. xiii. 1
(O.S. III. 448.7–10).   [36] II. iii. 8 (O.S. III. 282.8–9).   [37] I. xvi.
2 (O.S. III. 188.31–32).   [38] I. xvi. 5 (O.S. III. 195.18–26).
[39] I. xvii. 3 (O.S. III. 205–6).   [40] I. xvii. 1 (O.S. III. 202.6, 12–13).

[41] I. xvii. 11 (O.S. III. 215.8–10).   [42] I. xiv. 4 (O.S. III. 156.-
18–21).   [43] I. xiv. 11 (O.S. III. 162–63).   [44] II. v. 5 (O.S. III.
302–3).   [45] II. v. 9 (O.S. III. 317.14–15).   [46] II. xvii. (O.S. III.
508–15).   [47] II. xvii. 3 (O.S. III. 511.7–9).   [48] IV. i. 9 (O.S. V.
13.24–26).   [49] III. ii. 14 (O.S. IV. 24.34–25.5).   [50] III. ii. 14
(O.S. IV. 25.16–17).

[51] Com. Rom. 10:10 (C.O. 49.202).   [52] III. ii. 6–20 (O.S. IV.
13–30).   [53] Com. Ezek. 16:62 (C.O. 40.397).   [54] III. ii. 14 (O.S.
IV. 25.22–23).   [55] II. v. 5 (O.S. III. 303).   [56] Com. Jn. 12:29
(C.O. 47.293).   [57] III. ii. 16 (O.S. IV. 26.39–27.1).   [58] III.
ii. 16 (O.S. IV. 27.2–3).   [59] III. ii. 16 (O.S. IV. 26.29–32).
[60] Com. II Cor. 5:1 (C.O. 50.60–61).

[61] Com. Heb. 4:12 (C.O. 55.49–50).   [62] III. xvii. 1 (O.S. IV.
252.20–24).   [63] IV. xvii. 11 (O.S. IV. 354.11–15).   [64] IV. xvii.
11 (O.S. IV. 354.15–19).   [65] A few sample illustrations of Calvin's
use of the scripture for this kind of instruction are: Com. Gen. 49:8
(C.O. 23.597); Com. Ps. 9:9–12 (C.O. 31.101); Com. Ps. 19:7 (C.O.
31.199); Com. Luke 1:1 (C.O. 45.7); Com. Matt. 11:2 (C.O. 45.-
299); Com. Matt. 27:51 (C.O. 45.782).   [66] Com. II Tim. 3:17
(C.O. 52.384).   [67] Paul Tillich, *The Protestant Era,* p. xvi.
[68] *Ibid.*

Chapter VII

[1] Com. Ps. 69:28 (C.O. 31.650).   [2] II. viii. 8 (O.S. III. 350).
[3] II. viii. 8 (O.S. III. 350. note *c*).   [4] Com. Ex. 20:13; Dt. 5:17

(C.O. 24.611). ⁵ Com. Ex. 20:7 (C.O. 24.559). ⁶ Com. Num.
14:24 (C.O. 25.202). ⁷ Cf. Com. Lev. 21:17 (C.O. 24.456) ; Com.
Num. 30:1 (C.O. 24.572) ; Com. Dt. 27:15 (C.O. 25.8) ; Com. Ps.
19:1 (C.O. 31.194) ; Com. Ps. 45:10 (C.O. 31.457) ; Com. Matt.
15:10 (C.O. 45.452) ; Com. Matt. 19:18 (C.O. 45.538–39). ⁸ Com.
Matt. 28:8 & par. (C.O. 45.798). ⁹ Com. Matt. 27:44 & par. (C.O.
45.772). ¹⁰ Cf. Com. Luke 24:34 (C.O. 45.811) ; Com. Matt. 21:2
(C.O. 45.573) ; Com. Ex. 27:1 (C.O. 24.418).
¹¹ Com. Gen. 30:37 (C.O. 23.417). ¹² Com. Gen. 35:28 (C.O.
23.475). ¹³ C.O. 40.76. ¹⁴ Com. Ezek. 4:4–8 (C.O. 40.110).
¹⁵ Com. Ex. 9:2 (C.O. 24.109). ¹⁶ C.O. 24.197. ¹⁷ Com. Matt.
6:16 (C.O. 45.203–4). ¹⁸ IV. xvi. 20 (O.S. V. 324–25). ¹⁹ IV.
xvi. 30 (O.S. V. 335). ²⁰ Com. Isa. 27:13 (C.O. 36.460).
²¹ Com. Jer. 32:36, 37 (C.O. 39.36–37). ²² Com. Isa. 35:1
(C.O. 36.590–91). ²³ Com. Hosea 1:10 (C.O. 42.217). ²⁴ Com.
Obad. 19, 20 (C.O. 43.198). ²⁵ Com. Jn. 12:2 (C.O. 47.277).
²⁶ Com. Dt. 17:14 (C.O. 24.369). ²⁷ Com. Matt. 20:29; Mark
10:46; Luke 18:35 (C.O. 45.560). ²⁸ Com. Joshua 14:1 (C.O.
25.521). ²⁹ Com. Gen. 25:1 (C.O. 23.343). ³⁰ Com. Gen. 6:3
(C.O. 23.115) ; Com. Gen. 11:27 (C.O. 23.169–70; Com. Gen. 15:12
(C.O. 23.217–18) ; cf. Com. Ezek. 4:4–8 (C.O. 40.108) ; Com. Matt.
14:5 (C.O. 45.431–32).
³¹ Com. Matt. 28:1ff; Mark 16:1ff; Luke 24:1ff (C.O. 45.793) ;
Com. I Cor. 15:5 (C.O. 49.538–39). ³² Com. Joshua 23 (C.O.
25.559). ³³ Com. Matt. 21:10ff; Mark 11:11ff (C.O. 45.579).
³⁴ Com. Gen. 7:2 (C.O. 23.129). ³⁵ Com. Jonah 3:10 (C.O. 43.-
260) ; Com. II Peter 1:10 (C.O. 55.449) ; Com. Ps. 18:20 (C.O.
31.180). ³⁶ III. iii. 21 (O.S. IV. 80.11–19) ; Com. Heb. 6:4 (C.O.
55.70–71). ³⁷ Com. Dt. 6:13 (C.O. 24.561). ³⁸ Com. Jer. 7:21
(C.O. 690–91). ³⁹ Com. Joel 3:17 (C.O. 42.597). ⁴⁰ C.O.
52.251–52; cf. III. xxiv. 15 (O.S. IV. 427.17–21) ; III. xxiv. 16 (O.S.
IV. 428.29–31).
⁴¹ Cf. Com. Gen. 17:7 (C.O. 23.237) ; Com. Dt. 1:9 (C.O. 24.-
190) ; Com. Ps. 19:8 (C.O. 31.201) ; Com. Isa. 23:18 (C.O. 36.396) ;
Com. Hosea 14:1, 2 (C.O. 42.498) ; Com. Luke 1:18 (C.O. 45.18–
19) ; Com. Jn. 1:21 (C.O. 47.21) ; Com. Jn. 7:39 (C.O. 47.182) ;
Com. I Jn. 2:18 (C.O. 55.321) ; Com. James 1:27 (C.O. 55.396–97).
⁴² Julius Schniewind, "A Reply to Bultmann," in Bartsch, *Kerygma
and Myth: A Theological Debate,* p. 45. ⁴³ Com. Hosea 11: 8, 9
(C.O. 42.442). ⁴⁴ Com. Matt. 26:39 (C.O. 45.722). ⁴⁵ Com.
Gen. 11:7 (C.O. 23.166). ⁴⁶ Com. Ps. 10:1 (C.O. 31. 108–9) ; cf.
Com. Matt. 23:37 (C.O. 45.644). ⁴⁷ Com. Gen. 3:21 (C.O. 23:77–

78).   ⁴⁸ Com. Gen. 32:24 (C.O. 23.442).   ⁴⁹ Com. Ex. 3:4 (C.O. 24.37).   ⁵⁰ Com. Ps. 98:3 (C.O. 32.48); Com. Ex. 6:5 (C.O. 24.79); Com. Ex. 2:23 (C.O. 24.34); Com. Gen. 8:1 (C.O. 23.135).   ⁵¹ Com. Gen. 2:2 (C.O. 23.32).   ⁵² Com. Jer. 26:17–19 (C.O. 38.533); Com. Gen. 6:6 (C.O. 23.118).   ⁵³ Com. Hosea 5:15 (C.O. 42.316–17).   ⁵⁴ Com. Ps. 44:23 (C.O. 31.447–48).   ⁵⁵ Com. Dt. 5:29 (C.O. 24.207–8).   ⁵⁶ Com. Gen. 8:21 (C.O. 23.139).   ⁵⁷ Com. Dt. 32:19 (C.O. 25.367).   ⁵⁸ Com. Matt. 8:9 (C.O. 45.236–37).   ⁵⁹ Com. Ps. 2:4–6 (C.O. 31.44).   ⁶⁰ *Ibid.*

⁶¹ Com. Ps. 35:2 (C.O. 31.346).   ⁶² Com. Joshua 5:14 (C.O. 25.463–64).   ⁶³ Cf. Com. Ex. 3:2 (C.O. 24.35–36).   ⁶⁴ Com. Gen. 18:2 (C.O. 23.250–51).   ⁶⁵ Com. Jn. 4:1 (C.O. 47.77).   ⁶⁶ *Ibid.* ⁶⁷ J. Huizinga, *The Waning of the Middle Ages,* p. 14.   ⁶⁸ Com. Matt. 26:39 (C.O. 45.721).   ⁶⁹ Com. Matt. 26:37 (C.O. 45.720). ⁷⁰ Com. Jn. 11:33 (C.O. 47.265).

⁷¹ Com. Jn. 11:33 (C.O. 47.266).   ⁷² Com. I Cor. 13:5 (C.O. 49.511).   ⁷³ Com. Matt. 6:25–30; Luke 12:22–28 (C.O. 45.209). ⁷⁴ See Reinhold Niebuhr, *An Interpretation of Christian Ethics* and *The Nature and Destiny of Man.*   ⁷⁵ Com. Matt. 5:24 (C.O. 45.181–83).   ⁷⁶ Com. Rom. 1:9 (C.O. 49.15); cf. Com. James 5:12 (C.O. 55.429–30).   ⁷⁷ C.O. 45.179–80.   ⁷⁸ Com. Matt. 5:38 (C.O. 45.-183–84).   ⁷⁹ Com. Matt. 5:40 (C.O. 45.185).   ⁸⁰ *Ibid.*

⁸¹ Com. Matt. 5:42; Luke 6:34 (C.O. 45.186).   ⁸² *Ibid.* ⁸³ Com. Matt. 19:20 (C.O. 45.539).   ⁸⁴ Com. Luke 3:10 (C.O. 45.119–20).   ⁸⁵ Com. Matt. 10:37; Luke 14:26 (C.O. 45.294). ⁸⁶ Com. Matt. 7:1 (C.O. 45.213).   ⁸⁷ Com. Jn. 8:11 (C.O. 47.190–91).   ⁸⁸ *Ibid.,* col. 191.   ⁸⁹ Com. Jn. 8:7 (C.O. 47.190). ⁹⁰ Com. Matt. 13:24 (C.O. 45.368).

⁹¹ Com. Matt. 7:1 (C.O. 45.214), italics mine.   ⁹² C.O. 40.86. ⁹³ Com. Jer. 12:5 (C.O. 38.134).   ⁹⁴ *Ibid.,* col. 135.   ⁹⁵ C.O. 38.217.   ⁹⁶ *Ibid.*   ⁹⁷ *Ibid.,* col. 218.   ⁹⁸ *Ibid.*   ⁹⁹ Com. Jer. 15:19 (C.O. 38.233).   ¹⁰⁰ Com. Jer. 20:7 (C.O. 38.341).

¹⁰¹ Com. Jer. 20:14–16 (C.O. 38.352–54).   ¹⁰² Com. Ex. 2:12 (C.O. 24.26–27).   ¹⁰³ Com. Jer. 18:21 (C.O. 38.314).   ¹⁰⁴ Com. Ps. 7:6 (C.O. 31.82).   ¹⁰⁵ Com. Ps. 17:1 (C.O. 31.159). ¹⁰⁶ Com. Ps. 69:28 (C.O. 31.650); Com. Obad. 19, 20 (C.O. 43.198); Com. Gen. 17:7 (C.O. 23.237); Com. Gen. 8:1 (C.O. 23.135). ¹⁰⁷ Com. Zech. 1:7–11 (C.O. 44.138); Com. Ex. 25:2 (C.O. 24.399); Com. Dt. 24:16 (C.O. 24.631); Com. Gen. 7:2 (C.O. 23.129); Com. Matt. 21:10ff (C.O. 45.579); Com. Gen. 17:7 (C.O. 23.237); Com. Hosea 14:1, 2 (C.O. 42.498); Com. Gen. 6:6 (C.O. 23.118). ¹⁰⁸ Com. Zech. 1:7–11 (C.O. 44.138); Com. Obad. 19, 20 (C.O. 43.198); Com. Joel 2:28 (C.O. 42.567); Com. Hosea 11:8–9 (C.O.

42.442) ; Com. Gen. 11:5 (C.O. 23.166).   [109] Com. Ex. 20:4 (C.O. 24.376) ; Com. Isa. 27:13 (C.O. 36.460) ; Com. Joel 3:17 (C.O. 42.597) ; Com. Luke 1:18 (C.O. 45.18–19).

Chapter VIII

[1] III. xxiv. 1 (O.S. IV. 410.23–25).   [2] III. ii. 16 (O.S. IV. 410.23–25).   [3] Com. Rom. 8:34 (C.O. 49.165).   [4] III. ii. 14 (O.S. IV. 25.22–23).   [5] Com. Jn. 10:28, 29 (C.O. 47.250).
[6] Dedication to the *Institutes,* Allen, p. 24 (O.S. III. 13.18–21).
[7] II. x. 2 (O.S. III. 404.18).   [8] IV. viii. 9 (O.S. V. 140.19–141.11).
[9] I. xiv. 1 (O.S. III. 152.12).   [10] III. xxi. 3 (O.S. IV. 371.35–372.3).
[11] See IV. i. 21 (O.S. V. 25.3–6).   [12] Com. Rom. 8:16 (C.O. 49.150).   [13] I. xvi. 5 (O.S. III. 195.24–26).   [14] I. vii. 1 (O.S. III. 65.5–16).   [15] I. vii. 4 (O.S. III. 70.15).   [16] I. vii. 5 (O.S. III. 70.17).   [17] More complete accounts of this incident may be found in John T. McNeill, *The History and Character of Calvinism,* pp. 168ff; Williston Walker, *John Calvin,* pp. 288–91.   [18] See McNeill, *The History and Character of Calvinism,* p. 172; Walker, pp. 315–23.
[19] III. ii. 4 (O.S. IV. 12.21–22).   [20] III. ii. 17 (O.S. IV. 27.25–32).
[21] *Ibid.,* lines 32–34.   [22] III. ii. 18 (O.S. IV. 29.7–12).   [23] III. ii. 18 (O.S. IV. 29.19–20).   [24] III. ii. 18 (O.S. IV. 29.21–24).
[25] Com. I Peter 1:5 (C.O. 55:211).   [26] Dowey, *The Knowledge of God in Calvin's Theology,* p. 192.   [27] III. xxi. 1 (O.S. IV. 369.35).
[28] III. ii. 11 (O.S. IV. 21.7–9).   [29] Com. Eph. 3:12 (C.O. 51.183).
[30] III. xiv. 5 (O.S. IV. 223.19–21).
[31] Com. Jn. 6:63 (C.O. 47.159).   [32] I. vi. 2 (O.S. III. 63.11–12).   [33] IV. x. 8 (O.S. V. 170.13–21).   [34] Com. Gen. 3:6 (C.O. 23.60–61).   [35] Com. Acts 2:23 (C.O. 48.40).   [36] Com. Jn. 5:42 (C.O. 47.126).   [37] Com. Jn. 13:6 (C.O. 47.306).   [38] Com. Ps. 73:16 (C.O. 31.682).   [39] Com. Ps. 62:11 (C.O. 31.591).   [40] Com. Ps. 19:7 (C.O. 31.200).
[41] Com. Psalms, Author's Preface (C.O. 31.21 [Latin], 22 [French]).   [42] I. xviii. 4 (O.S. III. 227.27–30).   [43] Com. Jer. 23:36 (C.O. 38.452).   [44] Com. Gen. 3:6 (C.O. 23.61–62).   [45] IV. i. 5 (O.S. V. 8.9–11).   [46] Com. Heb. 8:11 (C.O. 55.104).   [47] Com. Heb. 8:10 (C.O. 55.102).   [48] Com. Luke 24:45 (C.O. 45.816–17).
[49] Com. I Thess. 2:13 (C.O. 52.151).   [50] Com. Jn. 15:10 (C.O. 47.343).
[51] Com. Jer. 7:21–24 (C.O. 37.692).   [52] Com. Rom. 1:5 (C.O. 49.11).   [53] Com. Acts 3:8 (C.O. 48.65).   [54] Com. I Jn. 2:3 (C.O. 55.311).   [55] Com. Jer. 31:33 (C.O. 38.690–91).

Epilogue

¹ Carl F. H. Henry, *The Drift of Western Thought*, p. 122.
² Henry, *The Protestant Dilemma: An Analysis of the Current Impasse in Theology*, p. 55.   ³ E. J. Carnell, *An Introduction to Christian Apologetics*, p. 174.   ⁴ *Ibid.*, pp. 200–201.   ⁵ Karl Barth, *The Doctrine of the Word of God: Church Dogmatics*, Vol. I, Part I, p. 155.   ⁶ *Ibid.*, p. 181.   ⁷ *Ibid.*, p. 170.   ⁸ *Ibid.*, p. 126.   ⁹ *Ibid.*, pp. 127–28.   ¹⁰ Karl Barth, *The Doctrine of the Word of God*, Vol. I, Part II, p. 463.

¹¹ *Ibid.*, p. 501.   ¹² *Ibid.*, p. 507.   ¹³ *Ibid.*, p. 509.   ¹⁴ Barth, *The Doctrine of the Word of God*, Part I, p. 120.   ¹⁵ *Ibid.*, p. 121.   ¹⁶ Barth, *The Doctrine of the Word of God*, Part II, p. 537.   ¹⁷ *Ibid.*, p. 513.   ¹⁸ *Ibid.*, pp. 585–659.   ¹⁹ *Ibid.*, p. 657.   ²⁰ *Ibid.*, p. 659.

²¹ Barth, *The Doctrine of the Word of God*, Part I, pp. 126–27.   ²² Barth, *The Word of God and the Word of Man*, p. 73.   ²³ Barth, "Continental vs. Anglo-Saxon Theology," p. 203.   ²⁴ Reinhold Niebuhr, "An Answer to Karl Barth," p. 235.   ²⁵ Barth, *Die Kirchliche Dogmatik, Band II, Die Lehre von Gott*, Zweiter Halbband, p. 401.
²⁶ *Ibid.*, p. 403.   ²⁷ Friedrich Gogarten, *Demythologizing and History*, p. 10.   ²⁸ Bultmann, *Jesus Christ and Mythology*, p. 36; cf. p. 17.   ²⁹ *Ibid.*, pp. 71–72.   ³⁰ Bultmann, *Essays Philosophical and Theological*, "Grace and Freedom," p. 176.

³¹ Bultmann, *Glauben und Verstehen*, Erster Band, "Kirche und Lehre im Neuen Testament," pp. 176, 177.   ³² Bultmann, *Jesus Christ and Mythology*, p. 71n.   ³³ Bultmann, *Theology of the New Testament*, Vol. I, p. 191.   ³⁴ Bultmann, *Jesus and the Word*, p. 8.
³⁵ Bultmann, *Jesus Christ and Mythology*, p. 53.   ³⁶ Bultmann, *Essays Philosophical and Theological*, "The Problem of Hermeneutics," p. 256.   ³⁷ *Ibid.*, pp. 255–56.   ³⁸ Bultmann, *Jesus and the Word*, p. 11.

Bibliography

SOURCES

Ioannis Calvini opera quae supersunt omnia, ed. by G. Baum, E. Cunitz, E. Reuss. 59 vols. (Corpus Reformatorum.) Brunsvigae, Schwetschke, 1863–1900.
Calvini opera selecta, ed. by P. Barth, G. Niesel. 3 vols. Monachii, Kaiser, 1926–36.

TRANSLATIONS

Calvin: Theological Treatises, translated with introductions and notes by J. K. S. Reid (*The Library of Christian Classics,* Vol. XXII). Philadelphia: The Westminster Press, 1954.
The Commentaries of John Calvin, various translators, 46 vols. Edinburgh: The Calvin Translation Society, 1843–55.
Institutes of the Christian Religion, translated by John Allen. 7th ed., revised. 2 vols. Philadelphia: The Board of Christian Education, 1936.
Tracts of Calvin; with his life by Theodore Beza, translated by Henry Beveridge. 3 vols. Edinburgh: The Calvin Translation Society, 1844–51.

LITERATURE

Bainton, Roland H., *The Reformation of the Sixteenth Century.* Boston: The Beacon Press, 1952.
Barth, Karl, "Continental vs. Anglo-Saxon Theology," *The Christian Century,* LXVI (1949), 201–4.
———, *The Doctrine of the Word of God (Church Dogmatics,* Vol. I, Part I), translated by G. T. Thompson. Edinburgh: T. & T. Clark, 1936.
———, *The Doctrine of the Word of God (Church Dogmatics,* Vol. I, Part II), translated by G. T. Thompson and Harold Knight. Edinburgh: T. & T. Clark, 1956.

————, "How My Mind Changed, 1938–1948," *The Christian Century*, LXVI (1949), 298–300, 333–34.

————, *Die Kirchliche Dogmatik*. Band II, *Die Lehre von Gott*, Zweiter Halbband. Zurich: Evangelischer Verlag A. G. Zollikon, 1946.

————, *The Word of God and the Word of Man*, translated by Douglas Horton. London: Hodder and Stoughton Limited, 1928.

Barth, Peter, *Das Problem der natürlichen Theologie bei Calvin*. München: Chr. Kaiser Verlag, 1935.

Bartsch, Hans Werner, editor, *Kerygma and Myth*, translated by Reginald Fuller. New York: The Macmillan Company, 1953. London: S.P.C.K., 1954.

Bauke, Hermann, *Die Probleme der Theologie Calvins*. Leipzig: Verlag der J. C. Hinrichs'schen Buchhandlung, 1922.

Berger, Peter L., "Demythologization—Crisis in Continental Theology," *The Review of Religion*, XX (1955), 5–24.

Binns, L. Elliott, *The Reformers and the Bible*. Cambridge: W. Heffer and Sons Ltd., 1923.

Blake, Eugene Carson, "The Character of Religious Authority in Protestantism," *The Journal of Religious Thought*, V (1948), 15-25.

Brauer, Jerald C., "Francis Rous, Puritan Mystic." Unpublished doctoral dissertation, University of Chicago, 1949.

Breen, Quirinius, *John Calvin: A Study In French Humanism*. Grand Rapids, Michigan: Wm. B. Eerdmans Publishing Company, 1957.

————, "John Calvin and the Rhetorical Tradition," *Church History*, XXVI (1957), 3–21.

Brunner, Emil, *The Christian Doctrine of Creation and Redemption (Dogmatics*, Vol. II), translated by Olive Wyon. Philadelphia: The Westminster Press, 1952.

————, *The Christian Doctrine of God (Dogmatics*, Vol. I), translated by Olive Wyon. London: Lutterworth Press, 1949.

————, *Revelation and Reason: The Christian Doctrine of Faith and Knowledge*, translated by Olive Wyon. Philadelphia: The Westminster Press, 1946.

Brunner, Peter, *Vom Glauben bei Calvin*. Tübingen: Verlag von J. C. B. Mohr (Paul Siebeck), 1925.

Bultmann, Rudolph, *Essays Philosophical and Theological*, translated by James C. G. Greig. New York: The Macmillan Company, 1955.

———, *Glauben und Verstehen,* Erster Band. Tübingen: Verlag J. C. B. Mohr (Paul Siebeck), 1933.

———, *Jesus and the Word,* translated by Louise Pettibone Smith and Erminie Huntress Lantero. New York: Charles Scribner's Sons, 1934.

———, *Jesus Christ and Mythology.* New York: Charles Scribner's Sons, 1958.

———, *Theology of the New Testament,* translated by Kendrick Grobel. 2 vols. New York: Charles Scribner's Sons, 1951, 1955.

Carnell, Edward John, *An Introduction to Christian Apologetics.* 4th rev. ed. Grand Rapids, Michigan: Wm. B. Eerdmans Publishing Company, 1952.

Clavier, Henri, *Études sur le calvinisme.* Paris: Librairie Fischbacher, 1936.

Cullmann, Oscar, "Scripture and Tradition," *Cross Currents,* III (1953), 262–77.

Dakin, A., *Calvinism.* London: Duckworth, 1940.

Davies, Horton, *The English Free Churches.* New York: Oxford University Press, 1952.

———, *The Worship of the English Puritans.* Philadelphia: Westminster Press, 1948.

Davies, Rupert E., *The Problem of Authority in the Continental Reformers.* London: The Epworth Press, 1946.

De Wulf, Maurice, *History of Medieval Philosophy,* translated by Ernest C. Messenger. 2 vols. London: Longmans, Green and Co., Ltd., 1926.

———, *An Introduction to Scholastic Philosophy: Medieval and Modern,* translated by P. Coffey. New York: Dover Publications, Inc., 1956.

Doumergue, E., *Jean Calvin: Les hommes et les choses de son temps.* Tome IV. Lausanne: Georges Bridel & Cie Éditeurs, 1910.

Dowey, Edward A., Jr., "Continental Reformation: Works of General Interest, Studies in Calvin and Calvinism since 1948," *Church History,* XXIV (1955), 360–67.

———, *The Knowledge of God in Calvin's Theology.* New York: Columbia University Press, 1952.

Dykstra, D. Ivan, "European Protestantism and the Bible," *The Christian Century*, LXII (1945), 1090–92.

Farrar, Frederic W., *History of Interpretation*. New York: E. P. Dutton and Co., 1886.

Ferguson, Wallace K., *The Renaissance in Historical Thought*. New York: Houghton Mifflin Company, 1948.

Ferm, Vergilius, editor, *The Protestant Credo*. New York: Philosophical Library, 1953.

Fitch, Robert E., "The Seat of Religious Authority," *The Journal of Religious Thought*, V (1948), 6–15.

Fullerton, Kemper, *Prophecy and Authority: A Study in the History of the Doctrine and Interpretation of Scripture*. New York: The Macmillan Company, 1919.

Gauteron, Ellis, *L'Autorité de la Bible d'après Calvin*. Montauban: Orphelins Imprimeurs, 1902.

Gerrish, Brian A., "Biblical Authority and the Continental Reformation," *Scottish Journal of Theology*, X (1957), 337–60.

Gilbert, George Holley, *Interpretation of the Bible, A Short History*. New York: The Macmillan Company, 1908.

Gilmore, Myron P., *The World of Humanism*. New York: Harper and Brothers Publishers, 1952.

Gilson, Etienne, *Christianity and Philosophy*, translated by Ralph MacDonald. New York: Sheed and Ward, 1939.

———, *God and Philosophy*. New Haven: Yale University Press, 1941.

———, *History of Christian Philosophy in the Middle Ages*. New York: Random House, 1955.

Gloyn, Cyril K., "Religious Authority and Modern Life," *The Journal of Religious Thought*, V (1948), 25–42.

Gogarten, Friedrich, *Demythologizing and History*, translated by Neville Horton Smith. New York: Charles Scribner's Sons, 1955.

Gray, James, "Authority of Scripture and Tradition," *The Shane Quarterly*, XIV (1953), 39–79.

Haller, William, *Liberty and Reformation in the Puritan Reformation*. New York: Columbia University Press, 1955.

———, *The Rise of Puritanism*. New York: Columbia University Press, 1938.

Harbison, E. Harris, *The Christian Scholar in the Age of the Reformation*. New York: Charles Scribner's Sons, 1956.

Harkness, Georgia, *John Calvin: The Man and His Ethics.* New York: Henry Holt and Company, 1931.

Hauck, Wilhelm-Albert, *Christusglaube und Gottesoffenbarung nach Calvin.* Gütersloh: Verlag C. Bertelsmann, 1939.

————, *Die Erwählten: Prädestination und Heilsgewissheit nach Calvin.* Gütersloh: Verlag C. Bertelsmann, 1950.

Henderson, Ian, *Myth in the New Testament (Studies in Biblical Theology,* No. 7). Chicago: Henry Regnery Company, 1952.

Henry, Carl F. H., *The Drift of Western Thought.* Grand Rapids, Michigan: Wm. B. Eerdmans Publishing Company, 1951.

————, *Fifty Years of Protestant Theology.* Boston: W. A. Wilde Company, 1949.

————, *Giving a Reason for Our Hope.* Boston: W. A. Wilde and Company, 1949.

————, *The Protestant Dilemma: An Analysis of the Current Impasse in Theology.* Grand Rapids, Michigan: Wm. B. Eerdmans Publishing Company, 1949.

————, *Remaking the Modern Mind.* 2d ed. Grand Rapids, Michigan: Wm. B. Eerdmans Publishing Company, 1948.

————, *The Uneasy Conscience of Modern Fundamentalism.* Grand Rapids, Michigan: Wm. B. Eerdmans Publishing Company, 1947.

Herzog, Frederick L., "Theologian of the Word of God," *Theology Today,* XIII (1956), 315–32.

Horton, Walter M., "Neo-Orthodox Conceptions of Biblical Authority," *The Journal of Religious Thought,* V (1948), 42–56.

Huizinga, Johan, *The Waning of the Middle Ages,* translator not listed. Garden City, New York: Doubleday and Company, Inc., 1954.

Hunter, A. Mitchell, *The Teaching of Calvin.* 2d ed., rev. Westwood, New Jersey: Fleming H. Revell Company, 1950.

Jansen, John Frederick, *Calvin's Doctrine of the Work of Christ.* London: James Clarke and Co., Ltd., 1956.

Kegley, Charles W. and Robert W. Bretall, eds., *The Theology of Paul Tillich (Library of Living Theology,* Vol. I). New York: The Macmillan Company, 1952.

Knappen, M. M., *Tudor Puritanism: A Chapter in the History of Idealism.* Chicago: The University of Chicago Press, 1939.

Knox, R. A., *Enthusiasm: A Chapter in the History of Religion.* New York: Oxford University Press, 1950.

Kolfhaus, Wilhelm, *Vom christlichen Leben nach Johannes Calvin.* Buchhandlung des Erziehungsvereins Neukirchen Kreis Moers, 1949.

Lehmann, Paul L., "The Reformers' Use of the Bible," *Theology Today*, III (1946), 328–44.

Lindsay, Thomas M., *A History of the Reformation.* 2 vols. 2d ed. Edinburgh: T. & T. Clark, 1907–8.

McKeon, Richard, "Renaissance and Method in Philosophy," *Studies in the History of Ideas*, III, 37–117, edited by the Department of Philosophy of Columbia University. New York: Columbia University Press, 1935.

McNeill, John T., *The History and Character of Calvinism.* New York: Oxford University Press, 1954.

———, "Thirty Years of Calvin Study," *Church History*, XVII (1948), 207–40.

Meeter, H. Henry, *Calvinism: An Interpretation of Its Basic Ideas.* 2d ed. rev. I. *The Theological and the Political Ideas.* Grand Rapids, Michigan: Zondervan Publishing House, n.d.

Menzies, Allan, *A Study of Calvin and Other Papers.* London: Macmillan and Company, Limited, 1918.

Miller, Perry, *The New England Mind: 17th Century.* New York: The Macmillan Company, 1939.

Neeser, Maurice, *Le Dieu de Calvin d'après l'Institution de la Religion Chrétienne.* Neuchâtel: Secrétariat de l'Université, 1956.

Niebuhr, H. Richard, *The Meaning of Revelation.* New York: The Macmillan Company, 1941.

Niebuhr, Reinhold, "An Answer to Karl Barth," *The Christian Century*, LXVI (1949), 234–36.

———, "Coherence, Incoherence and Christian Faith," *Union Seminary Quarterly Review*, VII (1952), 11–25.

———, *An Interpretation of Christian Ethics.* London: SCM Press, 1936.

———, *The Nature and Destiny of Man.* New York: Charles Scribner's Sons, 1953.

———, "We Are Men and Not God," *The Christian Century*, LXV (1948), 1138–40.

Niesel, Wilhelm, *The Theology of Calvin*, translated by Harold Knight. Philadelphia: The Westminster Press, 1956.

Noltensmeier, Hermann, *Reformatorische Einheit: Das Schrift-verständnis bei Luther und Calvin.* Graz-Köln: Hermann Böhlaus, 1953.

Nuttall, Geoffrey F., *The Holy Spirit in Puritan Faith and Experience.* Oxford: Basil Blackwell, 1946.

Nygren, Anders, "On the Question of De-Mythologizing Christianity," *The Lutheran Quarterly,* IV (No. 2, 1952), 140–52.

———, "Revelation and Scripture," *Theology Today,* V (1948), 318–27.

Parker, T. H. L., *The Doctrine of the Knowledge of God: A Study in the Theology of John Calvin.* Edinburgh: Oliver and Boyd, 1952.

———, *The Oracles of God: An Introduction to the Preaching of John Calvin.* London: Lutterworth Press, 1947.

Pauck, Wilhelm, *The Heritage of the Reformation.* Boston: Beacon Press, 1950.

Pfeiffer, Rudolph, "Humanitas Erasmiana," *Studien der Bibliothek Warburg.* Leipzig: B. G. Teubner, 1931.

Piper, Otto, "The Authority of the Bible," *Theology Today,* VI (1949), 159–74.

Prenter, Regin, *Spiritus Creator,* translated by John M. Jensen. Philadelphia: Muhlenberg Press, 1953.

Reid, J. K. S., *The Authority of Scripture: A Study of the Reformation and Post-Reformation Understanding of the Bible.* New York: Harper and Brothers, 1958.

Richardson, Alan, and Wolfgang Schweitzer, editors, *Biblical Authority for Today.* Philadelphia: The Westminster Press, 1951.

Ritschl, Otto, *Dogmengeschichte des Protestantismus.* III Band: *Orthodoxie und Synkretismus in der altprotestantischen Theologie (Fortsetzung) Die reformierte Theologie des 16. und des 17. Jahrhunderts in ihrer Entstehung und Entwicklung.* Göttingen: Vandenhoeck und Ruprecht, 1926.

Rylaarsdam, J. Coert, "Preface to Hermeneutics," *The Journal of Religion,* XXX (1950), 79–90.

Schlingensiepen, H., "Erasmus als Exeget. Auf Grund seiner Schriften zu Matthäus," *Zeitschrift für Kirchengeschichte,* XLVIII (1929), 16–57.

Schwarz, W., *Principles and Problems of Biblical Translation.* Cambridge: The University Press, 1955.

Seeberg, Reinhold, *Lehrbuch der Dogmengeschichte,* Vierte Band, Zweite Hälfte. Erlangen: A. Deichertsche Verlagsbuchhandlung Dr. Werner Scholl, 1920.

Smith, Ronald Gregor, "What Is De-mythologizing?" *Theology Today,* X (1953), 34–45.

Street, Thomas Watson, "John Calvin on Adiaphora: An Exposition and Appraisal of His Theory and Practice." Unpublished doctoral dissertation, 1958.

Stuermann, Walter E., *A Critical Study of Calvin's Concept of Faith.* Tulsa, Oklahoma, 1952.

Sykes, Norman, *The Crisis of the Reformation.* London: Geoffrey Bles, 1938.

Thomas, John Newton, "The Authority of the Bible," *Theology Today,* III (1946), 159–72.

Tillich, Paul, *Biblical Religion and the Search for Ultimate Reality.* Chicago: The University of Chicago Press, 1955.

———, *The Protestant Era,* translated and with a concluding essay by James Luther Adams. Chicago: The University of Chicago Press, 1948.

———, *Systematic Theology,* Vol. I. London: Nisbet and Co., Ltd., 1953.

Torrance, T. F., *Calvin's Doctrine of Man.* London: Lutterworth Press, 1949.

Van Til, Cornelius, *The Defense of the Faith.* Philadelphia: The Presbyterian and Reformed Publishing Company, 1955.

———, *The New Modernism: An Appraisal of the Theology of Barth and Brunner.* Philadelphia: The Presbyterian and Reformed Publishing Company, 1946.

Walker, Williston, *John Calvin: The Organizer of Reformed Protestantism, 1509–1564.* New York: G. P. Putnam's Sons, 1906.

Wallace, Ronald S., *Calvin's Doctrine of the Word and Sacrament.* Edinburgh: Oliver and Boyd, 1953.

Walvoord, John F., editor, *Inspiration and Interpretation.* Grand Rapids, Michigan: Wm. B. Eerdmans Publishing Co., 1957.

Warfield, Benjamin Breckinridge, *Calvin and Calvinism.* New York: Oxford University Press, 1931.

Wendel, François, *Calvin: Sources et Évolution de sa Pensée Religieuse*. Paris: Presses Universitaires de France, 1950.

Wernle, Paul, *Der Evangelische Glaube nach den Hauptschriften der Reformatoren*, III, *Calvin*. Tübingen: Verlag von J. C. B. Mohr (Paul Siebeck). 1919.

Williams, Daniel Day, *What Present-Day Theologians Are Thinking*. New York: Harper and Brothers, 1952.

Index

Abraham, 34, 61
Accommodation, 13f, 16, 55, 60, 107, 114, 115
Angels, 98, 139
Apostles' Creed, 24, 28, 67
Augustine, 25, 71

Barth, Karl, 6, 143ff
Bauke, Hermann, 3
Bilheimer, Robert S., 1
Bolsec, Jerome Hermes, 127
Brunner, Peter, 4, 54, 55
Bultmann, Rudolph, 112f, 149ff

Calvinist orthodoxy, 140ff
Carnell, Edward John, 50n, 142f
Castellio, Sebastian, 127
Certainty, 9, 16, 19f, 21, 28, 30, 123, 124ff
Christ: agent of God's grace, 67ff, 103, 105, 125, 136, 145, 149; anxiety of, 113; communion with, 104f; example of moderation, 116ff; humanity of, 96; key to the scriptures, 62, 64f, 147f; as Mediator, 91; necessity of union with, 67f; object of obedience, 24; in the Old Testament, 64, 147f; Old Testament prophecies dictated by, 53; prophecies of, 109f; as Redeemer, scriptural proof, 99; resurrection of, 96; as revelation of divine will, 92, 103; the soul of the Bible, 56f; as Teacher, 75
Christocentrism, 4

Church, the, 28ff, 100; authority of, 70f, 78f; object of belief, 28, 90f
Churches of Christ, the, 100n
Clavier, Henri, 5
Concupiscence, 11
Council of Trent, 81
Councils, the authority of, 79
Creation, 94

Daniel, 53
David, 51f, 61, 96, 122
Davies, Rupert E., 5
Demythologization, 112ff, 149f
Docility, 132ff
Doubt, 19, 126ff
Doumergue, Emil, 2f, 5, 54, 55
Dowey, Edward A., Jr., 4, 68n, 92, 129

Election, 36, 99, 127, 129f, 139
Ethics, 116ff
Evil, 34f
Ezekiel, 50f

Faith, 41ff, 90ff, 154f; anology of, 20, 81; implicit, 12f, 38, 90, 132f; justification by, 151
Francis I, 20, 26, 81
Free will, 99, 102
Fundamentalism, 142f

Galileo, 95
Gauteron, Ellis, 2
Gerrish, Brian A., 5, 50
God: beneficence, grace and mercy, 4, 62ff, 72f, 90ff, 99, 102ff, 128,